flāv'our favorites

beloved recipes from 10 years of cooking classes

flāv'our favorites

beloved recipes from 10 years of cooking classes

by denise norton

photographs by john caruso, carusophoto

design by tom deja, bossman graphics

createspace | charleston | 2014

Published in the United States by CreateSpace,
an Amazon Company, Charleston.

ISBN: 0692293094
ISBN 13: 978-0692293096

Manufactured in the
United States of America

First Edition

To my mother, who always supported me,
though she never got the chance to know me as a chef.
I miss you.

And to my partner, John, who has only known me as a
chef & who supports me in countless ways,
each & every day.

ACKNOWLEDGEMENTS

This book would not exist without Flavour students – our customers who have taken our cooking classes, shopped with us, come to our events, read our emails, eaten at our table & generally supported our culinary efforts. I am eternally grateful for your patronage, encouragement, stories, kindness & laughter (& for the chocolate chip cookies you bring in sometimes!). These past 10 years have been amazing & my little shop "down the street" has been a real source of community. "Thank you" is hardly enough to each of you wonderful students for helping me realize my dream, to live my truth.

A special thank you to all the students that agreed to test recipes in your own home kitchens. Your efforts were integral in clarifying the instructions in the recipes…to dot the i's & cross the t's, so to speak. Your comments were enlightening, helpful, funny & crucial to this process. Thanks for your participation & commitment. I hope we did your testing justice!

To the Flavour chefs & staff who worked directly on the cookbook…Chefs Renee, Ginna, Stephen, & Brian… Ms. Hansi (who was a tireless taste-tester every round – go girl!), Steffanie (snap!), Matthew & of course, Lauren (our intern-turned-chef!) for keeping me honest & organized. Testing days were AWESOME & this has been a crazy, fun-filled ride! To our other staff members who have supported the work around the cookbook… Chef Helge, Veronica, Joey, Jennifer, Laura, Geraldine, Julie, & young Will. Flavour is Flavour because you are you! Thanks for all of your commitment to the cause.

To Flavour John, aka John Caruso, our amazingly talented, upbeat, funny, beret-wearing photographer with an eye that creates magic. This book would truly not be what it is without the talent of your photography. From the first day we met (weird Christopher Walken t-shirt wearing dude) to your beautiful, enigmatic business card with a picture of a napkin dispenser on it that I saved on the bulletin board for almost nine months, it was really professional serendipity. Your

fierce energy, your enthusiasm-beyond-belief for testing day & unwavering dedication to getting the right shot have all been driving forces for this project. I can say no more about your absolute genius.

Tom, our designer & man behind the layout…thanks for making what was in my head come out on paper in such a beautiful manner. I am grateful for your patience, talent & level-headedness. You, sir, are a design wizard & your ability to interpret my vision is nothing short of remarkable.

Next, my partner John. You have been a part of Flavour ever since the speck of an idea became a reality. One day I'm buying paint at Paulson's to redecorate your office when I spy the "for rent" sign on the window across the street. A few short weeks later I've signed a lease. You have been a masterful ally in all things Flavour – from carpenter to taste-tester, from dishwasher to greeter, from light-bulb changer to confidant. I feel exceptionally blessed to have you by my side in this adventure. You never waver in your support & can always find a solution during the challenging bits. Thank you, my love, for being my rock. Oh, & for making ME dinner when I really need it!

Then there are the close friends & family who endure my craziness. Christine, who I've known since we were 12, was my original partner in founding Flavour & is the most passionate, wonderful being I know. My love & gratitude for your special humor, your caring calls, your resolute support & your kick-in-the-pants-when-I-really-need-it mentality. A voicemail from you & your laugh are all I ever need to set me right again.

Patsy & Vivi, a mother & daughter team that I can truly say made me a chef. I will never forget sitting in that bar in Toronto apprehensively telling you "I think I'm going to go to culinary school" amidst a great deal of obstacles. You both steadfastly supported, encouraged & resolutely told me I could do it. On top of you being my surrogate family, you are both wonderful, loving, giving, amazingly talented women who I am beyond proud to know & have in my life. Thank you for helping me become the person I am today & for supporting the accountant-turned-chef who wrote this book.

Rick & Rachel (Charlotte, too), Sue & Jeremy, Stacey & Bill, Susan V., Eric the Tall…my foodie friends who let me cook when I need to, who feed me when I need it, who fill the champagne glass when it gets empty & who encourage me in ways that only friends can do. You've tasted the goods, sat in seats for filming crazy things & cleaned my dirty dishes. Thank you! A special call out to Rachel, who not only champions my business every chance she gets, but who has also been integral in staging the scene that is Flavour with her brilliant work (chandeliers, drapery etc.). You're a great friend!

To my family, who live too far away: I pick on you (& sometimes I do this in front of my classes!), I don't call often enough, & I miss a lot of the seminal moments because I live here. Thank you for accepting me as I am, for always being interested in the weird stuff I do & for your texts when I'm on live tv & need to make sure I'm not making a fool of myself. You buoy me in so many ways even though you live farther away than I'd like. Much love to all of you.

Then, to a few lovely other people…Elizabeth Berg for always being a vocal supporter of Flavour & who has brought much wisdom & counsel to me over the years; Karen Doornebos who makes me feel special every time she opens her mouth; Michael Davis & Dacor for believing in me & endowing our kitchen with great equipment; & Lorne Golman & Perfect Cut Productions for putting together an amazing crew to get Flavour on film & who I hope to work with a lot more very soon.

And lastly, but certainly not least-ly, thank you to the most incredible chefs, staff & folks who have made up the Flavour team over the years. We have had many amazing people amongst our ranks. Chefs who cook, lead & instruct, people who associate our classes & help clean all of those dishes, personnel who wait on customers when they want to sign up for a class or make a purchase, & managers who do all the behind the scenes things that make the business run. The cumulative effect of your awesomeness has had a big part in the making of this cookbook. You wonderful people have come & gone throughout the years, but you come back to say hi, call, email & still support us. Thanks for your contributions!

INTRODUCTION

Growing up, my mother put dinner on the table every nite for our family, 6pm sharp. She & my dad both worked, like so many people do across America. She always cooked, but her repertoire was somewhat limited & the advent of convenience food had reached a heyday. There were the "hamburger assistance boxes", asparagus from a can, lots of casseroles with canned cream of chicken soup, meatloaf (oh, so much meatloaf) & the ever-popular "meat-za pie" (which was really just meatloaf in a pie pan, smothered with jarred spaghetti sauce & topped with shredded cheese). Despite some of the scars that I endured from these early childhood suppers, in retrospect, the family meal & gathering every nite at the dinner table seem idyllic.

I know for so many of you, this family togetherness is hard work now, with so much happening in our modern, technology-driven, fast-paced world.

When we opened the doors of Flavour Cooking School, just over 10 years ago, our hope & goal was to get people cooking more & eating together at the family table. Our mission...to teach fundamental cooking techniques & basic principles & to get people inspired to cook from scratch with real ingredients (no small task in this day & age of ever-present fast-food & convenience products).

Opening day was the beginning of December. One of our very first customers was the husband of a lovely woman who worked at our bank (so he'd heard about us from her as we were under construction). Let's call him "Mr. S". Well, Mr. S plunked down over $400 for a Christmas gift card for his wife so we could teach her how to cook (as I recall, there was some desperation in his eyes!). Mrs. S took her gift seriously & started classes right away. I found out that at Thanksgiving, the very next year (a mere 11 months later), her entire family raised a glass & toasted ME for teaching her how to cook! This story epitomizes what makes all of us at Flavour Cooking School tick.

Real ingredients, approachable dishes, family togetherness, & delicious food...that is what our shop & classes are all about & it's the underlying philosophy of this cookbook.

We've been teaching classes every day in our shop for the local community & helping our neighbors put home-cooked food on the table for years now. We've held parties, celebrated milestones & instructed kids how to make dishes from scratch. We couldn't be prouder when a customer comes in & tells us that our tres leches cake that she baked for her Mexican family was the tastiest they've ever had, or when a little tyke in our young chef's class says that the chicken soup he just helped cook was the best he's ever eaten in his whole life!

Over the years, guests have asked me "when are you going to write a cookbook?" so frequently that I've lost count. It's been a project in the back of my mind for ages, but, as you might imagine, the prospect is a bit daunting. About 18 months ago, I decided my New Year's resolution was to "just do it"...get started. You'd think with over 6,000 recipes in our repertoire that it would be easy. But then, how to choose? Which dishes? One day, we just started testing & taking pictures & before we knew it, things snowballed.

We've chosen our favorites from over the years...those recipes which we crave, that we teach over & over because they are good basics, the dishes that people request & the ones that we propose to a private party because we know they'll love them & go home to make themselves. We asked our students & got an impressive response with their number one go-to's. We're sorry we couldn't put them all in these pages. In fact, the response & requests could inspire future books!

This has been a true labor of love & I cannot express my gratitude for the words of encouragement from everyone (students, staff, family, etc.). We hope in some small way that the recipes in this book will inspire you to get in the kitchen & that they will become part of your family traditions. I'm sorry there is no meat-za pie here, but there is our meatloaf recipe (which I WISH my mom had known years ago!). We are proud of this work & these tasty recipes. We hope you use this cookbook often in your own kitchen.

Happy cooking!

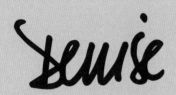

CONTENTS

A WORD ABOUT SALT

This is one of the most important sections of this book.

Again…this is one of the most important sections of this book! I'm hoping if I write it twice, it will catch your eye!

(Caveat: this section is not intended for those who have salt restrictions on their diet imposed by a doctor or who have chosen to be low-sodium for health reasons. We respect those of you who do not incorporate additional salt into your food for dietary & health reasons.)

We've curated this book of our favorite recipes from over 10 years of cooking classes – something over 4,000 classes, over 6,000 recipes & over 40,000 students. That's a lot to contemplate, huh? We've narrowed down the field into some pretty delicious dishes, we've cooked them a lot over the years in our classes, we've tested them each at least three times for this book & we've done a lot of tasting!

All that said, even the best-written, most well-researched, significantly tested recipe will likely be underwhelming to you without <u>some</u> salt.

Simply put, the "job" of salt in a recipe is to enhance the flavor of food. It brightens the essence of a dish, it facilitates harmony between the ingredients & it intensifies. Salt reduces bitterness, smoothes out acidity & enhances sweetness. It provides balance.

I purposefully don't put amounts of salt in many recipes because we all have different salt palates. Also, if you're cooking at home & use a different brand of an ingredient than we used in our dish during testing, that could widely vary the need for salt.

Our recipes are typically written:

tt   sea salt
tt   black pepper, freshly ground

where tt = to taste.

We ask that, as you cook from this book, you taste your dish & adjust the seasoning to your palate. This will require some judgment on your part. That said, most of the dishes in this book will likely need some seasoning.

In our "elements of flavor" class, we do a great tasting exercise that often drives the point home about how important salt can be to a recipe. I make a pot of soup with fresh broccoli & no-sodium chicken stock (straight from the recipe in this book called "cream of anything soup"). We taste the soup four times in class – one batch with no salt, one with a little salt, one with (in MY opinion) the <u>right</u> amount of salt & one that has too much salt. The soup tastes profoundly different as we progress. The first taste usually elicits derisive comments like, "this tastes like a pot of broccoli". The next batch with some salt gets a few yums. It's not until the 3rd taste that most people "get" what I'm saying. This third batch tastes not JUST like broccoli, but like a delicious, balanced, I-want-to-eat-more-of-this kind of soup. It's just right. When we then add too much salt, people can see the difference & comment that the last taste is over the top & the salt dominates the flavor.

A few tips on seasoning:

**salt sparingly as you cook
(add more at the end if needed)**
During the cooking process, many of our chefs season as they go (a bit on the meat in a sear, a bit in the liquid as it cooks, etc.). This does help blend the flavors in the recipe. Do so sparingly, however, so that any reduction in liquid doesn't result in an overly salty concentration. Remember you can almost always add more at the end to compensate, if needed.

taste, season, taste

Taste a portion of the finished dish. If you're not certain whether it needs more salt, take a bit out (into a ramekin or on a spoon) & sprinkle on a tiny bit of salt. Taste again. If it somehow now tastes better or more flavorful with this added salt, this is an indication to you to season the entire dish a bit more. I learned this "pull some out & season" method in culinary school & it did really help me to refine my tasting palate. You may not THINK something needs salt, but when you add just a tiny bit more, you'll find that the flavors pop!

less is more

Under-seasoning is the way to go. You can always add more salt after you've tasted it again, but you cannot take salt out once you've gone too far. Start sparingly & work your way to the right balance.

pre-existing salt conditions

Don't forget that some of the ingredients in a dish might have a salty pre-disposition (olives, capers, parmesan cheese, soy sauce, fish sauce, etc.). If you taste your dish first, you'll observe this, but don't forget to consider these salty components in your dish as you're finishing.

stop short (if you're not sure) & put salt on the table

If you're serving to a crowd & it feels like you might be adding a lot of salt, consider seasoning a bit less & putting the salt on the table. It is really true that we all have our own salt thresholds, so if you stop a bit under, then at least the dish won't come across as "too salty" to your guests.

and remember...

When you're cooking a dish & using all natural ingredients (like a salad), nothing has salt in it already. It may seem like you're adding a lot of salt to get the right final taste, but that amount of salt is likely a lot less than if you were eating prepared, packaged, pre-salted, preserved foods. Cooking from scratch & adding your own salt is almost always a much lower sodium proposition.

I conclude this section with an anecdote from one of our at-home testers. We gave her a soup recipe, with a variety of good, healthy, delicious ingredients. When we received her rating form, we were perplexed to read that she rated the dish just "so-so" & was not excited to make it again. She specifically said "I feel there is something else missing, but can't quite figure out what".

I sent her an email to find out more. Turns out, she is a very low salter (for health reasons) & as a result, tends not to season anything. After a few emails back & forth, it emerged that her stock choice was pretty salt heavy, BUT not seasoning the dish at the end made the rest of the flavors unbalanced. Had she used a lower sodium stock & seasoned to taste, there would have been more harmony in the finished soup (& less salt to boot). Each time during the at-home testing process that we got a lower-than-expected rating for taste, we found out that our testers had neglected to do the final step – seasoning "tt", or to taste, at the end.

The moral of the story...if you can't quite figure out what is missing...it's probably salt. If you've made a dish with good quality ingredients, put in the love, cooked it according to the recipe & it's still not quite right...try more salt!

You're SUPPOSED to taste as you cook, season as you go. It's a happy requirement of the process. Just use tasting spoons, please (& no finger licking!).

Stay salty, my friends!

RECIPES ARE A ROADMAP

With my "type A" personality, please believe me when I say that if I could write a recipe that answered all of your questions & put to rest all of your apprehensions, I absolutely would. It's my goal to get you cooking, so anything I can do to suppress anxiety is important. As a recovering perfectionist, former CPA, pretty green-around-the-gills culinary school student, I used to drive my instructors crazy with questions trying to drill down to the minutia of preciseness to get it right.

Only after asking this question a multitude of times… "how long does <u>that</u> take?" did the answer really finally sink in…

"When it's done"!

My mission now as a recipe writer & chef instructor is to do the best job possible to describe "what IS the doneness factor" & <u>approximately</u> how long that might take, time-wise, to get accomplished.

As a reader of this cookbook & hopefully a cook from it, you have to take a leap of faith. There are times when I will ask that you trust your gut. Read, then re-read, what the doneness factor is & then cook to achieve it.

These recipes are indeed roadmaps. There are indicators along the way to ensure you're on the right track (sauté til aromatic); measurements to take (teaspoons, cups, 1/8" thick); smells to smell; tastes to taste; & time to wait. However, if you are searing a piece of meat & it's not as brown as you'd like it to be even though you've cooked it the recommended 4-6 minutes, don't panic. Aim for what the recipe says, but also learn to trust yourself. The result will usually be very edible!

Here are just a few of the variables that can cause differences in timing:
- your oven is different than mine
- the flame on your stove has different btu's than mine
- your pans are smaller / bigger / different metal than mine
- your meat is colder or warmer than mine
- your onion is bigger than mine

…etc.

Cooking is art, not perfection. The beauty in nature of different sized cloves of garlic can cause panic for some when they are cooking with them (is THIS a lg clove of garlic?). Try as much as you can to "be one with the process" & enjoy the cooking progression as much as the outcome. If a recipe calls for a sm onion, can you use ½ of a lg one from your pantry? Sure. If the recipe tells you to dice a carrot & you don't have time so you grate it, is that ok? Probably. When you bake, a bit more preciseness should prevail. Accurately measuring the stated ingredients is usually key in the science that is baking, but cooking generally allows some leeway.

how to approach our recipes
We've laid out our recipes in this book in the same manner that we have done since our first class. Our die-hard fans have really responded to our recipe structure & we didn't want to "design-it-up" to make a fancy cookbook that diverted from our tried & true format.

The ingredients are all listed in one column on the left of each page. They are grouped according to how you work with them in the recipe, which should help facilitate your prep better (more on that in a bit). The cooking techniques are situated directly to the right of the ingredients. These techniques provide the cooking instructions related specifically to the ingredients they are next to in the recipe.

For example:

ingredients		techniques
1 T	extra virgin olive oil	*heat a lg sauté pan over med flame til hot
1	med onion, diced	*add oil & swirl to coat
		*add onion & sauté til tender, ~4-6 min
1	clove garlic, minced	*add garlic & sauté til aromatic, ~30 sec

The gap, or blank row, between sections (highlighted above with the dotted line), indicates a cooking "pause". In this example, once the pan has been heated, the oil added & onion sautéed, THEN move to the next phase & add the garlic. That gets sautéed til it's aromatic, which should only take about 30 seconds. THEN, move on to the next step.

Here is the perfect place to transition the discussion to prepping your ingredients.

mise en place

This would not be a Flavour cookbook if we did not elaborate on mise en place. This classic French phrase, literally translated, means "putting in place" or everything in it's place. In almost every class we teach we talk about it. It's not just a phrase, it's an over-riding culinary concept & principle.

If we had to "bullet-point" it, mise en place dictates that you:

*read the recipe
*make sure you have everything you need (ingredients AND equipment)
*get all your ingredients prepped, ready, cut & measured before you start cooking
*clean as you go – put things away
*cook with an eye towards doneness & properly cooking foods, not just for timing
*keep cleaning as you go
*be one with the food!

Taking the time to mise en place at the outset will end up saving you time in the long run. You're more organized, efficient & calmer when you cook. Plus, you're far less likely to do something accidently if you've properly mise en placed (now it's a verb) & everything is right where you need it.

With our recipes, we suggest you read them over first. THEN, prep all of the ingredients as written before you cook. Dice the onion, grate the carrot, dice the celery. If all of these ingredients are grouped together in the recipe, you can probably prep & put them all in one bowl. Make your way down the ingredient list & get each component fully prepped. THEN, start cooking. As you cook away, it will be more enjoyable as everything is within arms reach & ready to go.

After you've cooked the same recipe a time or two, you may be able to find time-saving spaces in the process, such as cutting or dicing some finishing ingredients during the long cook time for the main protein or similar situations. I often take notes in my cookbooks when I find the opportunity to make adjustments. Feel free to take your own notes & make your own adjustments to our roadmap.

about chef notes

Throughout the cookbook, we provide "chef notes" so that we can relay some of our class tips in the cookbook format. Certainly we cannot provide all of the guidance in a cookbook that we do when we teach a 2½ – 3 hour class. Our classes are designed to highlight & demonstrate the key concepts of a recipe AND to elaborate on the higher level cooking techniques involved. While we may not be able to do that all in this cookbook format, we hope that these recipes will be approachable & delicious nonetheless.

As you follow our roadmap, keep true to the concept of mise en place & do your best to enjoy the process as well as the final result. Cooking should be fun & we hope that this book can provide you with some straightforward guidance to make some mouthwatering & delectable dishes!

THE MAKING OF A COOKBOOK
...BEHIND THE SCENES

Each day of testing in the shop began with a mini-checklist (we LOVE our checklists at Flavour!). Turn on the ovens, pull out the measuring tape, print off the recipes, turn on the dishwasher, get out the recipe rating forms, find the scale...& coffee. Someone please make the coffee!

Since this is a book of our favorites, we knew that the recipes already worked & tasted delicious. In my mind though, it was not enough to simply take some "class recipes" & put them in a book for you. I really wanted to make sure that our instructions, timing, descriptions & measurements were as clear as we could possibly make them. Plus, I'm a (recovering) perfectionist!

Our testing protocol included three rounds: we tested in our kitchen, then asked students to test in theirs, & then we did the final test at Flavour again. We questioned our instructions, measured the thickness of the cuts & the doughs with a tape measure, & we even used extra thermometers in our ovens to make sure the temperatures were right. For this endeavor, we checked & cross-checked.

During each round, the food was cooked according to the recipe, tasted (which, of course, is the BEST part of testing) & rated by as many people as possible. Comments were taken into consideration & adjustments made. After each round, we made the necessary tweaks & moved forward to the next phase.

For the first round of testing in our kitchen at Flavour, there were usually two chefs, a scribe (who we probably should have called the "enforcer"), at least one more taste tester & our ever-so-talented photographer, John.

As we prepped, John would snap pictures of the process. Our scribe, usually Steffanie, would watch the chefs cook & confirm we were following the instructions to the letter. As the "enforcer", she was charged with

making sure we were not cooking from instinct, but that our actions mirrored what was written on the page. "Are you on a medium heat?", or "it's been 30 minutes...time to check the ovens", a lot of notes, writing & timing were all a part of her role in the process.

Once the dish was done, we tasted & rated. While this was such an enjoyable element of a testing day, it was also the most critical part too. Is the balance right? Does the food look appealing? If you were a guest, would you want to learn how to make this dish? We questioned everything we could think of, then put pen to paper.

All the while, John was there snapping away with one of his many cool cameras. Sure, he used some lights & sometimes there was that big silver screen for reflection. One of the things that I am most proud about this cookbook is that the shots you'll see inside these pages are the REAL food we cooked & ate. We did not wax anything or blow-torch food for a more golden color. We did not spritz things with water to make them glow. I will admit, a time or two, we put the prettiest charred vegetable on the top or we added a crumble or two to the foreground for "style". Those choices were to enhance the character of the picture, not to change the properties of the food. The pictures in this book are really as edible as they look!

Our student volunteers got the recipes for round II. We emailed instructions, a questionnaire & a recipe. We asked that they not contact us for advice, but rather cook the recipe as it was written. It was hard for some to refrain from asking us a question or two (we ARE a local cooking resource, after all). But, what we got back was a treasure trove of great work & insight. Some recipes went off without a hitch. A few others were somewhat problematic. Chilies & heat seemed to be a significant challenge for a few recipes & salting the dish at the end "to taste" another.

Because of their selfless (but delicious) work in their own kitchens, we've done our very best to provide more clarification for those recipes or sections that posed a challenge to our at-home testers. We even wrote the section in this book about salt as a result of their feedback. We genuinely thank our at-home testers & greatly appreciate their contributions to this book.

The last phase, round III at the shop, was the everything-really-should-be-right-at-this-point round, where we basically just cooked the recipe as written. We only took a few more notes at this point or tested a good correction found by our at-home testers. More tasting, more rating…then book it!

"Book it" sounds easy, but how does the recipe actually get from a word document in my computer to this lovely book? Enter our designer Tom & our awesome intern Lauren.

I met with Tom several times with our current portfolio of marketing materials. From those, he got the feel of our brand, then provided me with a few options on how to lay out the book. It actually was a difficult choice. But in the end, this book just felt like us. We collaborated on the recipe layout together & it was a several month process to get all of the recipes from my computer into his layout. From there it was…check alignment, oops, there are too many words on this page, the callout picture doesn't fit, the font here is different…lots of back & forth editing that finally put the puzzle together.

Our intern, Lauren, kept me organized through it all. She methodically compiled the folders that the recipe paperwork went in. She sent the recipes to our at-home testers & handled the correspondence with them. She researched our printing options & kept me on track. I think her official title should have been "the organizer" because without her efforts, I KNOW this book would have taken me six months longer!

At the end of this project, we've made a real printed cookbook! Many of you, I know, have binders of our Flavour recipes in your own kitchens that you use to cook from all the time. I guess those could be considered our "first" cookbook! But this one is "official"! This is for our students, fans & awesome customers who have been asking for 10 years for us to make one.

We sincerely hope you use the book, write notes in it, cook family meals from it & get a stain or two on its pages. That way we'll know it's been loved! We're very excited to bring these recipes to you, with gorgeous real food photography & a few chef notes & anecdotes to boot!

Now, stop reading & start cooking!

COOKBOOK RECIPE TESTING
IN PROCESS TODAY!!

FREE FOOD
in the shop NOW!

denise norton

APPETIZERS
& STARTERS

The introduction to this recipe reveals an embarrassing secret! This is a go-to dish for me when I have no food in the house (how can a chef have no food in the house?). I can usually scrounge up some bread, a can of white beans, a clove or two of garlic & a fresh herb somewhere. It's a tasty, filling accompaniment to a glass of white wine on the deck in the summer. We use this dish often in our elements of flavor class & vary the fresh herb so students can taste the subtle difference that each can produce in a dish. Next time you THINK you have no food in the house, try this!

WHITE BEAN CROSTINI
(makes 12-18)

ingredients

crostini
12-18	slices of french bread, thinly cut on a bias
2-4 T	extra virgin olive oil

white bean dip
2 T	extra virgin olive oil
1	15 oz can of cannellini beans, drained & rinsed
1	lg clove garlic, minced
1 t	minced fresh oregano OR rosemary OR dill
tt	sea salt
tt	black pepper, freshly ground

suggested additions when adding garlic
½ t	dried crushed red chili flakes OR
½ t	finely grated lemon zest OR
drizzle	fresh lemon juice OR
1 t	white wine vinegar

techniques
*preheat oven to 350°
*line a sheet pan with parchment paper

*brush both sides of bread lightly with oil
*place bread on sheet pan
*bake til golden & crisp, ~18-22 min

*heat a med sauté pan over med flame til hot
*add oil & swirl to coat
*add beans & garlic
*heat til beans are hot & garlic is aromatic, stirring often, ~1-2 min

*remove from heat & add herb of choice, S+P
*mash mixture with potato masher or fork
*taste & adjust seasoning
*thin with more olive oil, as needed
*spread white bean dip atop crostini
*serve warm

Try these suggested additions atop the finished crostini:
*crumbled blue cheese
*finely grated parmesan cheese
*baby arugula or spinach
thinly sliced red onion

This dish has been an obsession – I tasted its inspiration at a restaurant back when I was still an accountant in corporate america. Fast forward, & as a chef I was determined to "figure it out". Recently, I returned to that same restaurant, easily 15 years later. It was still on the menu. I confess I came pretty close with this recipe. As for why we call it "ridiculous", one or two bites & you'll know.

RIDICULOUS SMOKY CHEESE DIP
(makes ~2-3 c)

ingredients

1 c	grated sharp cheddar cheese
1 c	grated monterray jack cheese
1 c	grated fontina cheese
4 oz	cream cheese, softened
¼ c	quality mayonnaise
1-2 T	jalapeno juice (from jarred pickled jalapenos)
1	sm red pepper, cut into a very sm dice
~1 T	minced pickled jalapenos (from the jar)
4	scallions, finely minced
2-3 t	smoky paprika
tt	sea salt
tt	black pepper, freshly ground
some	celery ribs
some	baby carrots
some	tortilla OR pita chips

techniques

*put cheeses, mayo & 1 T jalapeno juice in the bowl of a food processor
*pulse several times to mix & cut cheeses into even smaller pieces

*add vegetables & smoky paprika to mixture
*pulse several times til thoroughly combined

*taste & adjust seasoning
*let sit ~30 min to blend flavors

*serve with celery, carrots & chips

chef notes

if this dip is made in advance, let the flavors blend in the refrigerator – then, make sure to take it out at least ~30 min before serving to bring the dip closer to room temp & to soften the texture

flavour recettes

This recipe combines two unlikely ingredients – avocado & blue cheese. Truth be told, I'm not a big blue cheese fan. That said, these flavors are so interesting together & with each bite, the heat sneaks up on you & it becomes more & more addictive. Each time we make this & serve it at a party or in a class, the compliments from our guests & students flow. Roq-on, my friends!

ROQUAMOLE

(makes ~2-3 c)

ingredients

2	ripe avocados, pit & peel removed
¼ c	roquefort OR blue cheese
½ c	sour cream
~2 T	minced pickled jalapenos (from a jar)
2	scallions, sliced thinly
2 T	minced fresh cilantro
¼ t	paprika
2-3 T	lime juice, freshly squeezed
tt	sea salt
tt	black pepper, freshly ground
some	celery ribs
some	baby carrots
some	tortilla chips

techniques

*put avocado flesh in a med bowl
*mash with potato masher or fork

*crumble blue cheese finely atop avocado
*add sour cream
*stir the mixture thoroughly to combine

*add jalapenos, scallions, cilantro & paprika
*stir thoroughly to combine

*add a bit of lime juice & stir thru
*taste & adjust seasoning & acidity

*serve with celery, carrots & tortilla chips

One of our tasters for this recipe commented, "I'd eat this sauce on everything"! That's exactly how we feel about it too. It's a spin on the traditional spanish tapas dish "chicken with romesco". We think everyone should be able to make a good roasted potato & we've crafted the sauce with some toasted pumpkin seeds for added flourish. Think chicken, pork chops or grilled salmon as other uses for the sauce – let your creative juices flow! ∽

ROASTED POTATOES
WITH PUMPKIN SEED ROMESCO
(serves 4-6)

<u>ingredients</u>

<u>techniques</u>
*preheat oven to 425°
*line a sheet pan with parchment paper

<u>roasted potatoes</u>
2 lbs   sm fingerling OR red potatoes

*wash & clean potatoes under cold water
*cut into ~1" bite size pieces
*place in a lg bowl & pat dry with towels

1-2 T   extra virgin olive oil

*drizzle 1 T of oil over potatoes
*toss potatoes to coat lightly with oil
*ensure that potatoes are just lightly covered, adding more oil as needed

½ t   fine sea salt
1 t   dried thyme

*add salt & thyme, tossing to coat
*place potatoes on prepared sheet pan
*roast in oven til golden & knife tender, ~30-40 min

<u>pumpkin seed romesco</u>
2-3   cloves garlic, peeled
¼ c   fresh parsley leaves

*turn on food processor (metal blade)
*add garlic & parsley thru the feed tube
*process til garlic & parsley are finely minced
*turn off food processor & scrape down sides

½ c   toasted shelled pumpkin seeds
1/3 c   diced day old french bread
1   roasted red pepper from a jar OR freshly roasted, peeled & seeded
1   med tomato, seeded
2 T   sherry vinegar
½ t   smoky paprika

*add remaining ingredients (except oil) to processor
*process til well combined

½ c   extra virgin olive oil
tt   sea salt
tt   black pepper, freshly ground

*turn on processor
*drizzle in oil slowly thru feed tube to emulsify
*taste & adjust seasoning
*too thick? add a bit of water OR vinegar (but make sure flavor remains balanced)
*too thin? add a bit more bread & process til minced
*serve with potatoes as a dipping sauce

These crispy crackers are irresistible. We liken them to the "adult" version of those supermarket cheesy, fish-shaped snacks (you know the ones we mean!). The cornmeal provides an interesting texture & the smoky paprika makes for a sophisticated flavor. They are easy to make & a tasty appetizer / snack for a party. What's better yet, is that you can make the dough & keep a portion of it in your freezer to have as quick, go-to for last minute guests (just make sure the dough is not frozen when you try to cut it!). The recipe makes quite a few, but ummmm....you might find yourself sneaking one here & there, so be warned!

CORNMEAL CHEDDAR ICEBOX CRACKERS

(makes ~ 7 dozen)

ingredients

2 c	flour
¼ c	yellow cornmeal (fine ground)
2 t	fine sea salt
1 t	smoky paprika
4 T	unsalted butter, chilled, cut in sm pieces
8 oz	finely grated extra sharp cheddar cheese (~2 c)
½ c	whole milk

techniques

*put dry ingredients into the bowl of a food processor
*pulse to combine

*add butter to processor
*pulse til mixture resembles coarse meal

*add cheese & pulse til combined

*turn machine on & immediately drizzle in milk quickly thru feed tube
*mix just til dough comes together in moist clumps (add up to 2 T more milk if it seems too dry)
*transfer to work surface
*gather dough & knead by hand several times to combine ingredients & smooth out dough
*shape dough into two separate ~2" wide logs, pressing to remove air pockets while shaping
*wrap with parchment paper OR saran wrap
*refrigerate til hardened, ~1 hr

*preheat oven to 325°
*line 2-3 sheet pans with parchment paper
*slice chilled logs thinly with a serrated knife into 1/8" rounds
*transfer crackers to sheet pan
*bake til crackers are lightly golden & firm in the center, ~25-35 min
*cool completely

Hummus from scratch becomes addictive. After you make & eat homemade hummus, you want to KEEP making it, varying it up & noshing on it, of course! All this recipe requires is a food processor & a few ingredients. In a jiff, this is a healthy, flavorful, yummy afternoon snack. We've made this smoky artichoke hummus for more parties than we can count & it's always met with "wow, I never realized hummus could taste SO good"! Served with carrots, celery & steamed veggies, here is a snack we can easily get behind.

SMOKY ARTICHOKE HUMMUS
(makes ~2 c)

ingredients

2	cloves garlic, peeled
¼ c	fresh parsley leaves

8-10	whole artichoke hearts, drained
1	15 oz cans of chickpeas (aka garbanzo), drained & rinsed
2-3 T	lemon juice, freshly squeezed
1-2 T	extra virgin olive oil
1 T	tahini (well stirred)
1 t	ground cumin
½-1 t	smoky paprika
tt	sea salt
tt	black pepper, freshly ground

some	celery ribs
some	baby carrots
some	pita chips

techniques

*turn on food processor (metal blade)
*add garlic & parsley thru the feed tube
*process til garlic & parsley are finely minced
*turn off processor & scrape down sides

*add artichokes, chickpeas, lemon juice, oil, tahini, cumin & paprika to bowl
*process til a smooth paste is formed
*thin, as necessary, with water OR lemon juice
*thicken, as necessary, with a bit more oil
*taste & adjust seasoning

*serve with celery, carrots & pita chips

chef notes
*many jarred artichokes are quartered – aim for ~12 – 14 oz of artichoke (which usually will equal ~8-10 whole hearts)

flavour favorites

Students are often intimidated by making shellfish dishes at home. Once we demo this in class & they taste the results, they're often inspired to give it a try. Most of the time, fresh mussels can be obtained at your local fishmonger & are relatively inexpensive compared to other seafood options. This dish is approachable, lusciously delectable & begs for a loaf of crusty bread to devour the leftover creamy sauce.

STEAMED MUSSELS IN WHITE WINE

(serves 4-6)

ingredients

1 T	unsalted butter
1	med shallot, minced
15 oz	can crushed or diced tomatoes OR 2 c fresh diced tomatoes
1 T	chopped fresh tarragon OR basil
½ c	dry white wine
2 lbs	mussels, scrubbed & debearded (mussels should be closed & alive)
½ c	heavy whipping cream
tt	sea salt
tt	black pepper, freshly ground

techniques

*heat a lg pot with lid over med flame til hot
*add butter & heat to melt
*add shallot & sauté til translucent, ~1-2 min

*add tomatoes, tarragon (OR basil) & wine
*bring to a boil
*reduce heat & simmer ~2-3 min

*add mussels & cover pot with lid
*steam til mussels completely open, ~3-5 min
*remove mussels from pot with tongs & place in serving bowl(s)
*discard any mussels that are not open

*add cream to pot & increase heat to hi
*boil til sauce thickens, ~2-4 min

*taste sauce & adjust seasoning
*ladle sauce over mussels
*serve immediately

 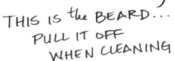

THIS IS the BEARD...
PULL IT OFF
WHEN CLEANING

CHIPPED =
NO GOOD!

CLOSED =
ALIVE

OPEN =
DEAD

Purchase & clean mussels right before you intend to cook them. They should smell fresh & salty, like the ocean. The mussels we eat are saltwater creatures, so during the cleaning process it's best not to hold them under running water. Instead, use a coarse, wet scrub brush to remove any grit. Then quickly pass the mussel under the water to rinse debris away.

As you clean & debeard the mussels, check to make sure their shells are tightly closed (indicating they are alive). Discard mussels with cracked shells. If any mussels are open, tap them gently on the counter & toss any that don't close quickly. Dead mussels should be discarded during the cleaning process as they may be unsafe to eat.

The place – the rustic french countryside & a charming maison nestled in the bucolic landscape. The hosts – aart & caroline (a most interesting dutch couple living in france!). The setting – a three hour al fresco meal in their picturesque garden with amazing friends & lots of french wine. The food – well let me just tell you this tart was only the first course of many for an unforgettable evening that ranks amongst my top meals of all time. This tomato tart, inspired by caroline, is memorable for so many reasons (one of our raters gave it 98.88 on a scale of 5!).

CAROLINE'S TOMATO TART
(serves 6-8)

ingredients

1	recipe cornmeal tart dough (next page)

drain/marinate tomatoes
4-6	garden ripe tomatoes, seeded & diced (need ~3 c diced tomatoes)
½ t	fine sea salt
1 t	herbes de provence

roll dough, fill & bake tart
some	flour

2 T	cornmeal (fine ground)
2 c	coarsely grated gruyère cheese

techniques

*prepare dough according to the recipe
*refrigerate til hardened, ~2-3 hrs

*place tomatoes in a colander set over a bowl
*add salt & herbes de provence to tomatoes & stir thru
*let sit for ~30-60 min for tomatoes to drain (stir occasionally)

*preheat oven to 375°
*line a sheet pan with parchment paper
*place metal quiche pan OR ceramic pie dish on sheet pan
*lightly dust work surface with flour
*roll cold dough to ~1/8" thick into a lg circle (lift & turn dough often so it won't stick)
*roll dough onto rolling pin
*lift & place dough into quiche pan OR pie dish
*gently lift & push dough to fit the pan
*allow excess to overhang

*sprinkle cornmeal evenly over tart bottom
*sprinkle on cheese, then tomatoes
*trim away edges (quiche pan) OR fold edges over filling (pie dish)
*bake til crust is golden & crisp, ~50-70 min
*let stand ~15 min, cut into wedges & serve

chef notes
*we have found the bake time to vary quite a bit for this tart – look for the edges to get golden & crisp (like a good pie), for the cheese to be beautifully melted, & for the tomatoes to be slightly dried out
*cornmeal comes in a variety of grinds – make sure to use a finer texture (closer to flour)
*we've even made this tart in a pinch without a pie dish or tart pan at all – we put the dough directly on the sheet pan, put the cornmeal, cheese & tomatoes on the dough with a ~1" border & folded the edges over

flavour favorites

This dough is heavenly & making it by hand is a throwback to simpler times. Several of our testers commented how approachable it is to make & everyone raves about its delectable taste. The cornmeal adds a lovely texture & I think overall it makes the crust a bit easier to roll & turn. The flavor & texture of the dough, plus beautifully ripe farmers market OR heirloom tomatoes, plus the gorgeous, melty gruyère cheese all adds up to summer tart nirvana!

CORNMEAL TART DOUGH

(makes dough for one ~9" tart)

ingredients

1 c	flour
¼ c	yellow cornmeal (fine ground)
1 t	sugar
1 t	fine sea salt
3 T	sour cream OR buttermilk, cold
1/3 c	cold water
7 T	unsalted butter, cold, cut into sm pieces

techniques

*put dry ingredients in a med bowl
*whisk to combine

*put dairy & water in a measuring cup &
  stir to combine
*refrigerate to keep cold

*add butter to dry ingredients
*use a pastry blender to cut butter into dry
  ingredients so pieces are ~the size of sm peas
*sprinkle the cold dairy/water mixture over dough
  (add ~3/4's), mixing with a fork to distribute
  (dough should be moist enough to stick
  together – if not add dairy mixture ~ 1 T at a time
  to create a soft, malleable dough)
*press into a disc (~3/4" thick) & wrap in
  plastic wrap
*refrigerate til hardened, ~2-3 hrs

In french cuisine, a gougère is defined a savory baked pastry made with choux paste dough mixed with cheese. Technically, this recipe IS a gougère, but it has a few elements that make it feel & taste like a pop-over. So we've renamed them gougère-overs! These little cheesy, flavorful puffs are not only a great appetizer by themselves BUT they can be also cut in half & stuffed with various fillings (think chicken salad OR mini-sandwiches). They'll disappear quickly, however you serve them!

CHEDDAR & MUSTARD GOUGÈRE-OVERS

(makes ~3 dozen)

<u>ingredients</u>

<u>techniques</u>
*preheat oven to 400°
*line 2-3 baking sheets with parchment paper

½ c	whole milk
½ c	water
½ t	fine sea salt
8 T	unsalted butter

*put milk, water, salt & butter in med saucepan
*heat over med hi flame & bring to a boil
*boil til butter melts

| 1 c | flour |

*add flour all at once
*stir with a wooden spoon til mixture forms a paste
*cook, stirring, for ~30 more sec
*remove from heat

| 5 | eggs |

*start a hand mixer on med speed in the dough
*add eggs one at a time
*mix well after each addition

8 oz	grated sharp cheddar cheese (~2 c)
2	scallions, minced
2 T	spicy brown OR dijon mustard

*add cheese, scallions & mustard
*mix well to combine
*scoop, spoon OR pipe batter onto baking sheets into ~1½" rounds, spacing ~2" apart
*bake til golden & crispy & inside is almost dry, ~30-35 min
*let cool
*eat warm OR room temp

f chef notes
*if you want to use these gougère-overs as a vehicle for food (to fill OR stuff them), consider baking them a tad longer to dry out the inside a bit more

SOUPS

This is a recipe fundamental – we teach this (or versions of it) in almost every soup class we host. It illustrates three classic soup thickeners – potato (pureed releases starch), vegetables (pureed themselves create thickness), & heavy cream. It's as delicious as it is illustrative. Now it's just up to you to choose WHICH vegetable to use!

CREAM OF ANYTHING SOUP

(serves 8-10)

ingredients

1½ lbs broccoli OR asparagus OR carrots, etc.
   (see chef notes)

2 T	unsalted butter
1	med onion, diced

2	cloves garlic, minced
1 t	dried thyme

1	lg idaho potato, peeled OR scrubbed clean & cut in ½" dice
6 c	chicken stock

¼-½ c heavy whipping cream

tt	sea salt
tt	black pepper, freshly ground

techniques

*peel & cut vegetables into 1" chunks
 (include stem if using broccoli, but peel it)

*heat a lg soup pot over med hi flame til hot
*add butter & heat to melt
*add onion & sauté til tender, ~4-6 min

*add garlic & thyme
*sauté til garlic is aromatic, ~30 sec

*add cut vegetables & potato & stir thru
*add stock, increase heat to hi & bring to a boil
*reduce heat to a simmer & cover
*cook til vegetables & potatoes are knife tender
 (time will depend on vegetable, ~20-30 min)
*remove from heat
*puree soup with an immersion blender, blender
 OR food processor til smooth

*return soup to pot
*add cream & heat thru

*taste & adjust seasoning

chef notes

*prepare this soup using other vegetables instead of broccoli: asparagus, carrots, mushrooms, cauliflower, corn, OR spinach
*when using a blender or food processor to puree soups, work in batches, fill the device only ~1/3rd full & cover the top with a kitchen towel to avoid any leaking - hot liquid expands as it is processed so it's important to exercise caution
*our retail director hansi likes to add sriracha OR tabasco to this soup for a little "kick"

denise norton

This soup, to me, is the asian version of chicken noodle soup...comforting, nourishing & oh, so delicious! The sambal provides the heat to the sour of the rice vinegar. Add vegetables & eggs & this soup begs to be devoured. We have been teaching this soup in our fundamentals classes over 10 years & a few years back, my dear friend rachel won her block party soup-off contest with this recipe – a real winner!

HOT & SOUR SOUP

(serves 8-10)

ingredients

8 c	chicken stock
1 T	finely grated fresh ginger
1/3-½c	soy sauce
1/3 c	rice vinegar
¼ c	cold water
3 T	cornstarch
2	eggs
6 oz	tofu, diced into ¼" pieces
6	scallions, cut in ¼" slices
2 c	thinly sliced napa cabbage
1 T	sesame oil
1-2 t	sambal (heat dependant)
2 T	minced fresh cilantro

techniques

*put stock & ginger in a lg heavy soup pot
*bring to a boil
*reduce heat & simmer to blend flavors, ~10 min

*place soy, rice vinegar, water & cornstarch in a sm bowl (this is called a slurry)
*mix well to combine
*add slurry to stock & bring to a boil

*break eggs into a sm bowl
*whisk with a fork to combine
*slowly drizzle eggs into pot using a fork to move eggs around soup to break them up

*add tofu, scallions, cabbage & oil to pot
*heat thru ~2 min
*turn off heat

*add sambal (start with a sm amount & add more to taste & desired heat level)
*taste & adjust seasoning & balance (use soy for salt)

*portion soup into serving bowls
*garnish with cilantro

chef notes

*the best tool to use for the ginger is a microplane – peel the fresh ginger, grate, then give the grater a swift tap on the counter to release the ginger from the underside

*sambal is a spicy asian condiment made with chilies & salt (& often vinegar) – the heat provided can be pretty intense, so start with a smaller amount & add more to your taste

*consider adding ~1 c of cooked chicken or pork to the soup OR add 1 lb of sm raw shrimp with the tofu & simmer til translucent & cooked thru, ~3 min

This soup has been a staple in our flavour recipe file since we opened our doors. One of the consistent comments we get is how much BETTER this soup tastes than canned tomato soup. That feedback always reminds me why we do what we do...delicious food is entirely within our reach. Quality ingredients + a little cooking know how = tasty dish (without chemicals, preservatives OR too much salt). We dare you to try this one!

ITALIAN BREAD & TOMATO SOUP

(serves 8-10)

ingredients

croutons
3 c	day old french bread, cut into ~½-1" cubes
3-4 T	extra virgin olive oil
tt	sea salt
tt	black pepper, freshly ground

soup
2 T	extra virgin olive oil
2	carrots, peeled & grated
2	celery stalks, diced small
1	med onion, diced
3	cloves garlic, minced
1 c	dry white wine
1	28 oz can of crushed tomatoes
4 c	chicken stock, lightly flavored
1 t	dried oregano
½ c	heavy whipping cream
½ c	sour cream
tt	sea salt
tt	black pepper, freshly ground
8-10	basil leaves, cut in a chiffonade

techniques
*preheat oven to 375º
*line a sheet pan with parchment paper

*place bread in a mixing bowl
*drizzle oil over bread & season with S+P
*toss thru to coat bread evenly
*place bread in 1 layer on sheet pan
*bake til golden & crispy, ~10-15 min

*heat a lg pot over med flame til hot
*add oil & swirl to coat
*add carrots, celery & onion to pot
*sauté til partially tender, ~5-7 min

*add garlic & sauté til aromatic, ~30 sec

*add wine & deglaze pot (scrape bits off bottom)
*increase heat to hi
*heat til most of the wine has evaporated, ~5-8 min

*add tomatoes, stock & oregano
*bring to a boil, then reduce heat to a simmer
*simmer, stirring occasionally, til vegetables are tender, ~15 min
*remove from heat

*add cream & sour cream
*puree soup with an immersion blender, blender OR food processor til smooth
*taste & adjust seasoning

*portion soup into serving bowl(s)
*top with croutons & garnish with fresh basil

chef notes
when using a blender or food processor to puree soups, work in batches, fill the device only ~1/3rd full & cover the top with a kitchen towel to avoid any leaking - hot liquid expands as it is processed so it's important to exercise caution

Who doesn't love chicken noodle soup? Each time we make this it's like a slice of americana wafting through the shop (or my house!). It is super satisfying to cook the chicken & make the stock from scratch. However, if you don't have time, a prepared stock & a good quality store bought chicken will do the trick. Don't skimp on the fresh dill – it really makes it homey. You don't have to have a cold or the flu to enjoy this deliciousness!

CLASSIC CHICKEN NOODLE SOUP

(serves 8-10)

<u>ingredients</u>

2 T	extra virgin olive oil
1	med onion, diced
2	carrots, cut into ½ moons, ~½" thick
2	celery stalks, cut in ½ lengthwise & cut into ½" thick slices
3	cloves garlic, minced
1 t	dried thyme
1	bay leaf
8-10 c	chicken stock (see chef notes)
4 oz	thin dried egg noodles
2 c	diced OR shredded cooked chicken meat (~2 sm chicken breasts)
¼ c	fresh parsley leaves, roughly chopped
1 t	minced fresh dill
tt	sea salt
tt	black pepper, freshly ground

<u>techniques</u>

*heat a lg soup pot over med flame til hot
*add oil & swirl to coat
*add onion, carrots & celery
*sauté til vegetables are partly softened, but not browned, ~3-4 min

*add garlic & dried herbs
*sauté til aromatic, ~1 min

*add chicken stock & bring to a boil

*add noodles & boil til al dente, ~5-8 min

*reduce heat
*add chicken & simmer to heat thru, ~2-3 min

*add parsley & dill & heat thru, ~1 min
*remove bay leaf
*taste & adjust seasoning

chef notes

*see next recipe "cooked chicken with easy homemade chicken stock" if you want to make your own light stock for this soup & to cook your own chicken
*make this a quick weeknite soup by using a prepared stock & a no-salt added roasted chicken from your grocer

denise norton

57

This recipe is really the companion for "classic chicken noodle soup" on the previous pages, but you can certainly use it to make your own stock for other dishes. This varies slightly from a classic stock recipe as we're suggesting you cook a whole chicken in the liquid instead of just using chicken bones. If you put a whole chicken in the liquid, in addition to the stock, you'll have cooked chicken meat that is both tender & succulent. Chicken soup, anyone?!

COOKED CHICKEN WITH EASY HOMEMADE CHICKEN STOCK

(makes ~4 c cooked chicken & ~16 c of chicken stock)

ingredients

3-4 lb	whole chicken (preferably free range)
3	celery stalks, cut into 1" chunks
2	lg white onions, peeled cut into 1/8ths
1	lg carrot, peeled & cut into 1" chunks
1	head of garlic, top 1/3 cut off to expose cloves & root trimmed to clean up
2	bay leaves
1 t	whole black peppercorns
1	sprig fresh thyme
6	fresh parsley stems with leaves

techniques

*discard any chicken innards
*rinse chicken with cold water
*place chicken in a lg stockpot
*add just enough cold water to cover, ~4 q (16 c)

*add remaining ingredients to pot
*bring to a boil over med hi heat
*reduce heat to a low simmer
*simmer til chicken is fully cooked & broth is flavorful, ~1½ - 2 hrs
*skim any impurities / foam off top during cooking
*add a bit more water as needed to keep meat covered
*remove chicken to cutting board
*remove skin & discard
*remove meat & shred OR dice into sm cubes
*strain stock carefully to remove solids & use stock for soup OR other recipes

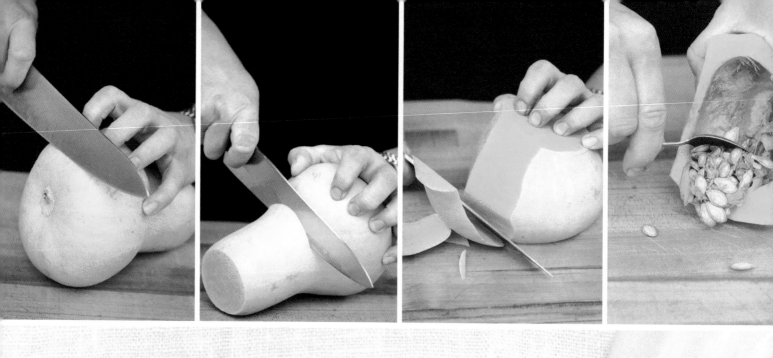

This dish scores high marks on all counts & is definitely one of our top recipes in the soup department! The lightly sweet squash, the slight bitter of the spinach, the tang of the wine & the salt & spice from the sausage create a tempting balance of the major flavors. We usually convert squash skeptics as each spoonful beckons another spoonful & before you know it, you're having another bowl.

SPICY ITALIAN SAUSAGE & BUTTERNUT SQUASH SOUP

(serves 6-8)

ingredients

1 T	extra virgin olive oil
1 lb	med spicy raw italian sausage (bulk) OR casings removed if links
1 T	extra virgin olive oil
1	med onion, diced
1	butternut squash, peeled, seeded & cut in a 1" dice (~1½ lbs of squash)
4	cloves garlic, minced
¼-½ t	dried crushed red chili flakes
1 t	packed dark brown sugar
½ c	dry white wine
4 c	chicken stock
½ t	dried ground sage
1	sm red pepper, diced
2 c	packed baby spinach
tt	sea salt
tt	black pepper, freshly ground

techniques

*heat a lg heavy soup pot over med hi flame til hot
*add oil & swirl to coat
*add sausage
*break sausage up with a wooden spoon & cook til browned & cooked thru, ~7-10 min
*remove meat & drain in paper towel lined bowl

*add more oil to pot as needed
*add onion & squash
*sauté til onion is almost tender, ~4-6 min

*add garlic, chili flakes & brown sugar
*stir thru & sauté til aromatic, ~30-60 sec

*add wine & deglaze pot (scrape bits off bottom)

*add stock & sage to pot
*bring to a boil, then reduce heat to a simmer
*simmer til squash is tender, ~15-20 min
*puree soup with an immersion blender, blender OR food processor til smooth
*return soup to pot over med flame

*add pepper & spinach
*heat til spinach wilts & pepper is al dente, ~5 min
*add reserved sausage & heat thru
*taste & adjust seasoning

chef notes

when using a blender or food processor to puree soups, work in batches, fill the device only ~1/3rd full & cover the top with a kitchen towel to avoid any leaking - hot liquid expands as it is processed so it's important to exercise caution

This tasty soup is a perfect base for using vegetables that are in your fridge OR if your eyes were bigger than your larder at the farmers market! You can most definitely vary the produce you use & the flavors are unmistakenly (& scrumptiously) asian. Whenever I eat this, I can FEEL the nutrition & healthfulness permeate my being – it is the epitome of the word nourish. Easy to make, wholesome & pretty, too. Don't be afraid, just dive in! ✑

NOURISHING ASIAN VEGETABLE UDON SOUP

(serves 4-6)

ingredients		techniques
1 T	fine sea salt	*bring a lg pot of water to a boil *add salt
6 oz	udon noodles	*cook noodles using the pasta method (lg pot, boiling water, salt, cooked al dente) *drain & rinse noodles in cold water
2 t	sesame oil	*drizzle noodles with oil & toss to coat *set aside
6 c 1 t 1 4 2 T	chicken OR vegetable stock packed dark brown sugar star anise ¼" chunks fresh ginger, peeled soy sauce	*put stock, sugar, anise, ginger & soy in a lg soup pot *bring to a boil *reduce to a simmer *simmer to blend flavors, ~10 min *remove star anise & ginger pieces
4 c 2	fresh vegetable combo, bite-size pieces such as: -bean sprouts -pea pods -shiitake mushrooms -thinly sliced zucchini OR yellow squash -thinly sliced red pepper -finely grated carrots heads of baby bok choy, thinly sliced	*add vegetable combo & bok choy *cook til vegetables are al dente, ~3-4 min *taste & adjust seasoning (use soy for salt) *add noodles to warm thru
1 2 T	lime, cut into wedges minced fresh cilantro	*portion out soup into serving bowls *serve with lime & garnish with cilantro

Our at-home tester admitted to us that she was a bit disappointed when she saw this recipe in her email inbox (we think she wanted something a bit more exotic!). Dutifully, she tested it AND she was rather overjoyed with the result. She thinks it's one of her favorite soups from flavour (& she's been to a lot of classes)! This soup is hearty, healthy & intensely satisfying with the addition of the barley. Sometimes, when you least expect it...

GRILLED VEGETABLE BARLEY SOUP WITH GREENS

(serves 8-10)

ingredients

barley
1 c	quick cook barley
some	water OR chicken stock OR vegetable stock (see pkg for proper hydration)
½ t	dried crushed red chili flakes

vegetables
2	sm zucchini or yellow squash, sliced into ½" planks
½ lb	asparagus, dry ends trimmed off
1	med white onion, sliced in ¼" slices
1	red pepper, cut into planks
~1 T	extra virgin olive oil

soup
8 c	chicken OR vegetable stock
1 t	dried thyme
1	bay leaf
1	lg bunch of greens (collard, mustard, chard, kale etc), stems removed & greens cut in sm pieces (~4-6 c), washed
1 c	finely grated parmesan cheese
2 t	white wine vinegar
1-2 T	lemon juice, freshly squeezed
tt	sea salt
tt	black pepper, freshly ground

techniques

*cook barley using the rice method WITH chili flakes
-barley + water/stock + chili flakes in a med pot
-bring to a boil
-turn down heat immediately to low
-cover with a lid & cook til tender

*heat grill pan or grill over med flame til hot
*brush vegetables with olive oil (both sides)
*grill vegetables til grill marks form & texture is al dente, ~2-4 min / side (time will depend on veggies)
*remove vegetables from grill, cool slightly & cut in ½" pieces (OR, alternatively, cut into lg chunks, place in a food processor & pulse to create a chunky mixture)

*place stock, thyme & bay in a lg soup pot
*bring to a boil

*add greens & cook til almost wilted, ~3-4 min

*add cooked barley, grilled chopped veggies & cheese
*add vinegar & lemon juice
*heat thru, ~2-3 min
*remove bay leaf
*taste & adjust seasoning

This recipe comes from one of our flavour fundamentals classes & it illustrates an essential cooking concept – making good quality soup from scratch can be SUPER easy! This hearty dish takes less than thirty minutes to make & is both satisfying & tasty. It can be eaten "whole bean" or pureed for a creamier texture. The main point is – make it soon & delight in your ability to cook something so scrumptious & rewarding!

BLACK BEAN SOUP

(serves 6-8)

<u>ingredients</u>

1 T	extra virgin olive oil
1	med white onion, diced
½ -1	jalapeno pepper, diced very sm (heat dependant)
3	15 oz cans of black beans, drained & rinsed
4 c	chicken OR vegetable stock
1 t	ground cumin
2-3 T	lime juice, freshly squeezed
½ c	fresh cilantro leaves, roughly chopped
tt	sea salt
tt	black pepper, freshly ground
6-8 T	sour cream
½	red pepper, cut into very sm dice (brunoise)

<u>techniques</u>

*heat a lg soup pot over med flame til hot
*add oil & swirl to coat
*add onion & sauté til translucent, ~3-5 min

*add jalapeno & sauté 1 min

*add beans, stock & cumin
*bring to a boil
*reduce heat
*simmer to blend flavors, ~10-15 min
*remove from heat
*puree soup, fully or partially, with an immersion blender, blender OR food processor

*add lime juice & stir thru
*stir in cilantro (reserve some for garnish)

*taste & adjust seasoning

*ladle soup into serving bowls
*garnish with sour cream, pepper & cilantro

🔲 chef notes

when using a blender or food processor to puree soups, work in batches, fill the device only ~1/3rd full & cover the top with a kitchen towel to avoid any leaking - hot liquid expands as it is processed so it's important to exercise caution

This soup answers the question..."what should I do with leftover turkey"?! For the record, we have successfully used turkey deli meat, cut in thick slabs & then diced, during the off-season. One of our testers remarked, "the tastes are unexpected but welcome – the fennel is a dandy addition & the mild heat level is like a fun surprise". Woo & hoo!

TURKEY TORTELLINI SOUP

(serves 8-10)

ingredients		techniques
2 T	extra virgin olive oil	*heat a lg soup pot over med flame til hot
1	sm onion, diced	*add oil & swirl to coat
1	red pepper, diced	*add vegetables
1	lg carrot, peeled & grated	*sauté to release flavors, ~3-4 min
2	stalks celery, diced sm	
3	cloves garlic, minced	*add garlic, fennel, oregano & chili flakes
2 t	fennel seeds	*stir thru
1 t	dried oregano	*sauté til aromatic, ~1 min
½ t	dried crushed red chili flakes (optional)	
7 c	chicken stock	*add stock
		*bring to a boil
		*reduce heat to a simmer
		*simmer til veggies are almost tender, ~6-8 min
8 oz	fresh OR frozen cheese tortellini	*bring soup back to a boil
1	sm zucchini, julienned thinly & cut into ~2" lengths (see page 127)	*add tortellini & zucchini
		*cook til pasta is tender, ~3-5 min (check tortellini pkg for cook time)
1 lb	smoked OR roasted turkey meat, diced in ¼" pieces	*add turkey, spinach & zest
4 c	baby spinach leaves	*stir gently & heat thru, ~1 min
¼ t	finely grated lemon zest	*taste & adjust seasoning
tt	sea salt	
tt	black pepper, freshly ground	
8-10	basil leaves, cut in a chiffonade	*ladle into serving bowls
some	fresh parmesan shavings	*garnish with basil & parmesan

denise norton

69

SALADS

We paid $13 for this delicious salad at a famous chicago steakhouse a few years ago. Admittedly, it was absolutely addictive & perfect for a rich steak dinner – crisp & creamy, light & full of good-for-you ingredients, & very nicely balanced. As we happily ate away, we started to dissect the ingredients & realized we could buy everything for less than $13 to serve a whole dinner party of people. So, of course, we had to figure it out & share with you!

STEAKHOUSE CHOPPED SALAD WITH WHITE BALSAMIC VINAIGRETTE

(serves 6-8)

ingredients

white balsamic vinaigrette

2 T	white balsamic vinegar
1-2 T	lemon juice, freshly squeezed
2 t	dijon mustard
1	clove garlic, pressed
1 T	minced fresh parsley
1/3 c	extra virgin olive oil
tt	sea salt
tt	black pepper, freshly ground

salad

2-3	romaine lettuce hearts, julienned in sm 1" pieces, rinsed & spun dry (~8 c)
½	sm red onion, diced sm
2	carrots, peeled & grated
2	stalks celery, diced sm
2	ripe avocados, diced sm
tt	sea salt
tt	black pepper, freshly ground

techniques

*put vinegar, lemon juice, mustard, garlic & parsley in a sm bowl
*whisk til combined

*drizzle in olive oil slowly while whisking
*taste & adjust seasoning (& oil/acid balance)

*put salad ingredients in a lg serving bowl
*season lightly with S+P
*add a portion of dressing & toss thru
*add more dressing as needed
*taste & adjust seasoning

We realized that one of the reasons this salad at the steakhouse was so tasty was that all of the ingredients were cut very small (every bite you take then bursts with multiple flavors). We also suggest that you not be afraid to salt the salad AND the dressing – doing so will help blend all of the ingredients, intensify the flavors & enhance the overall balance of the dish!

The lead in for this recipe has to be short since the recipe fills the page. You should know I make this dish multiple times during grilling season & the rustic croutons & creamy caesar dressing are an absolutely delightful flavor & texture combination!

RUSTIC CHICKEN CAESER SALAD

(serves 4-6)

ingredients

sear & roast chicken

4-6	chicken leg/thigh combos OR one whole chicken, cut into serving pieces
tt	sea salt
tt	black pepper, freshly ground

1 T	extra virgin olive oil
4 oz	diced pancetta

½	loaf of day old french bread, torn coarsely by hand to make ~1-2" lg rustic croutons (~4 c)
0-2 T	extra virgin olive oil
tt	sea salt
tt	black pepper, freshly ground
2 t	minced fresh rosemary

creamy caesar dressing

¼ c	finely grated parmesan cheese
2	anchovy fillets, drained & very finely minced
1	clove garlic, pressed
2 T	crème fraiche OR sour cream
2-3 T	lemon juice, freshly squeezed

1/3 c	extra virgin olive oil
tt	sea salt & black pepper, freshly ground

3	hearts of romaine lettuce, julienned thinly, cleaned & spun dry
¼ c	parmesan cheese, shaved

techniques

*rest meat at room temp for ~30 min while grill heats up
*heat grill OR grill pan til grates are hot
*season chicken generously with S+P
*place chicken on the grill, skin side down
*sear til grill marks form & skin is golden, ~6-8 min
*flip & sear underside, ~4-6 min
*remove chicken from grill

*heat a lg cast iron pot over med flame til hot
*add oil & swirl to coat
*add pancetta & cook til crispy, ~6-8 min
*remove pancetta from pan & set aside
*leave fat in pan

*remove pan from heat & add bread
*toss bread in fat & drizzle in olive oil as needed to lightly coat bread
*season with S+P & sprinkle rosemary over bread
*place chicken atop bread
*cover pot with a lid & place pan on grill indirectly (not right over open flame or coals)
*close grill lid to create oven effect (OR, place in a preheated 350° oven)
*roast til chicken internal temp reaches 165°, ~30-45 min (it could take longer depending upon grill temp)
*remove from grill/oven & rest ~10-15 min

*make dressing & salad while chicken is roasting
*put cheese, anchovies, garlic, crème fraiche & lemon juice in a sm bowl
*whisk ingredients together

*drizzle in oil while whisking constantly
*taste & adjust seasoning

*put lettuce in a lg serving bowl
*add a portion of dressing & toss to coat
*add more dressing as needed
*remove meat from bones & shred into bite-size pieces
*portion greens onto serving plate(s)
*top with meat & croutons
*garnish with pancetta & parmesan shavings

Quinoa is the "grain" with the funny name (pronounced keen-wah). It's been around for centuries, but has only recently gained mainstream prominence. Technically, it's a gluten-free seed that is cooked like a grain. Its major beauty lies in the delicious texture & flavor AND its incredible health benefits (high protein & fiber content). We've given quinoa a southwestern flair in this salad that could easily translate into a meal.

SOUTHWESTERN BLACK BEAN QUINOA SALAD

(serves 4-6)

ingredients

1 c	quinoa, rinsed (if needed)
1-2 c	vegetable OR chicken stock, OR water (check quinoa pkg for proper hydration)
1 c	frozen corn
1	15 oz can black beans, drained & rinsed
1	red pepper, diced sm
1	sm red onion, julienned
1	tomato, seeded & diced
½-1	jalapeno, seeded & minced
½ c	fresh cilantro leaves, roughly chopped
1	lime, zested
2 T	lime juice, freshly squeezed
½ t	ground cumin
2-3 T	grapeseed OR vegetable oil
1	clove garlic, pressed
tt	sea salt
tt	black pepper, freshly ground

techniques

*put quinoa & stock in a med saucepan
*bring to a boil, reduce heat to low & cover
*cook til liquid has absorbed, ~15-20 min

*remove from heat & add corn & beans
*let stand, covered, ~5 min
*heat over med flame til warmed thru if needed
*transfer quinoa to serving bowl

*add pepper, onion, tomato, jalapeno & cilantro to bowl

*add zest, lime juice, cumin, oil & garlic to bowl
*stir thru
*taste & adjust seasoning

chef notes

*most quinoa package instructions suggest a 2 to 1 hydration (two parts liquid to one part grain) – we find that this results in a "mushier" texture for the grain & generally we prefer to use a 1.5 to 1 ratio for a chewier, more al dente texture
*to help "control" the spice level, taste a sm bit of the jalapeno before adding it to the bowl
*try serving on a bed of lettuce to create a "cup"

This is not your typical salad...the name comes from the color of the components & the gorgeous green of the dressing. The flavor is herby & lightly tart, with a hint of sweet. We make this in classes to serve alongside heavier entrées – the crispness of the greens & cucumber are a perfect fresh foil to fatty or dense foods. The kohlrabi (or fennel) provides the unusual "wow" in each bite!

THE VERY GREEN SALAD

(serves 4-6)

ingredients

salad

½	english cucumber, cut in quarter-moon slices
2-3	romaine lettuce hearts, julienned in sm 1" wide pieces, rinsed & spun dry
½	white OR vidalia onion, julienned thinly into ~2" pieces
1	kohlrabi, peeled & thinly sliced OR 1 sm bulb of fennel, thinly sliced, then cut in ~2" pieces
tt	sea salt
tt	black pepper, freshly ground

vinaigrette

1	clove garlic, peeled
¼ c	loosely packed fresh parsley leaves
4-6	fresh tarragon leaves
12-15	fresh chives
½ t	fresh rosemary leaves
3 T	white wine vinegar
1 T	agave nectar (light) OR honey
2 t	dijon mustard
1/3 c	safflower, canola OR vegetable oil
tt	sea salt
tt	black pepper, freshly ground

techniques

*place salad ingredients in a lg bowl
*season greens lightly with S+P

*turn on food processor (metal blade)
*add garlic, parsley, tarragon, chives & rosemary thru the feed tube
*process til minced
*turn off processor & scrape down sides

*add vinegar, agave & mustard to processor

*turn on processor
*drizzle in oil slowly thru feed tube to emulsify

*taste & adjust seasoning (& oil/acid balance)
*add a portion of dressing to salad
*toss to coat
*add more dressing as desired

Sure, you can get ranch dressing out of a bottle, but there is such great satisfaction in making it yourself with ingredients that are fresh & real. Plus, this is a terrific recipe to make with kids as it's mostly measure, dump & mix. One comment we received during testing was, "I want to put this dressing on everything"! Frankly, we couldn't have said that better ourselves.

HOMEMADE RANCH DRESSING
(makes ~1½ c)

ingredients
1 c	quality mayonnaise
1/3 c	buttermilk
2	scallions, minced
2 T	minced fresh parsley leaves
2 T	minced fresh chives
1 T	minced fresh oregano
1	clove garlic, pressed
1 t	white wine vinegar
¼ t	celery powder OR seed
pinch	paprika
pinch	cayenne pepper
tt	sea salt
tt	black pepper, freshly ground

techniques
*place all dressing ingredients in a med bowl
*whisk to thoroughly combine
*refrigerate for ~30 min to develop flavors
*taste & adjust seasoning

DIY SALAD

suggested ingredients
some	lettuce (mesclun, romaine OR iceberg)
some	grated carrots
some	sliced celery
some	diced green OR red peppers
some	red onion matchsticks
some	diced english cucumber
some	black olives
some	grated cheddar cheese
some	cherry tomatoes, cut in ½
some	homemade ranch dressing

techniques
*place lettuce in serving bowl(s)
*top with your choice of vegetables

*add a portion of the dressing to salad
*toss to coat
*add more dressing as desired
*taste & adjust seasoning

chef notes
*this is a great dressing for summer (especially if you have an herb garden!) – dried herbs can be used, but since they are dehydrated (& thus their flavors concentrated), use ~1/3 as much (though, we do tend to prefer the overall flavor & texture of the fresh herbs in this dressing!)

denise norton

This salad perpetually earns "oohs" & "aahs". It has had many iterations throughout the years & the final jewel in the crown of its evolution was topping it with brie croutons (yep, you read that correctly!). In class, we often joke with guests that they should make a double batch of the croutons to ensure there are enough for the salad. We joke about it, but WE make a double batch when we make this at home! Just sayin'.

APPLE CIDER SALAD WITH BRIE CROUTONS

(serves 6-8)

ingredients

techniques
*preheat oven to 350°
*line a sheet pan with parchment paper

brie croutons
4-6 oz brie cheese

*remove rind from cheese with a serrated knife
*cut cheese in ~1" dice & place in a glass bowl
*microwave in ~20 sec bursts to melt, ~40-60 sec

2 T	extra virgin olive oil
2 c	day old french bread, cut into ½" cubes
tt	sea salt
tt	black pepper, freshly ground

*place oil in a lg mixing bowl
*add bread & melted brie
*season to taste with S+P
*toss bread with clean hands to thoroughly coat with oil & cheese
*place bread in 1 layer on sheet pan
*bake til golden & crispy, ~15-20 min
*remove from oven & let cool

warm vinaigrette
2 T	extra virgin olive oil
2	shallots, diced

*heat a sm fry pan over med flame til hot
*add oil & swirl to coat
*add shallot & sauté til tender, ~1-2 min

¼ c dry white wine

*add wine
*cook almost au sec (wine almost evaporated)

2 T	quality apple juice
1 t	apple cider vinegar
1 t	fresh thyme leaves, roughly chopped
tt	sea salt
tt	black pepper, freshly ground

*turn off heat
*stir in apple juice, vinegar & thyme
*taste & adjust seasoning (not too salty)

salad
4-6 c	baby spinach OR arugula greens (~5 oz)
2 T	lemon juice, freshly squeezed
1	granny smith apple, cored & thinly sliced
¼-1/3c	dried cranberries OR cherries

*place greens on serving plate(s)
*drizzle lemon atop greens
*spoon warm vinaigrette atop greens
*arrange apple & cranberries atop greens
*top with brie croutons

chef notes
*consider garnishing with 4-6 oz of cooked, crumbled bacon OR pancetta for even more decadence!

This is a classic salad found in many french restaurants. The poached egg winds up being part of the dressing & it's oh, so delish! When we make it, we generally prefer to put all of the eggs atop the entire salad & incorporate them thoroughly before serving, as it makes the dressing more integrated & creamy. Either way, all we can tell you is... make it soon!

BISTRO SALAD

(serves 6 as an appetizer, 4 as a dinner)

ingredients

techniques
*preheat oven to 375°
*line a sheet pan with parchment paper

croutons
2 c	day old french bread, cut in sm ½" cubes
1-2 T	extra virgin olive oil
tt	sea salt
tt	black pepper, freshly ground

*place bread in a med mixing bowl
*drizzle oil over bread & toss to coat (light coating of oil)
*season to taste with S+P
*place bread in 1 layer on sheet pan
*bake til golden & crispy, ~10-15 min

warm vinaigrette
4	bacon slices, cut into 1" strips

*place bacon in a cold sauté pan
*heat over med flame til crisp, stirring occasionally, ~10-15 min

1	shallot, diced

*add shallot & sauté til tender, ~30-60 sec

2-3 T	red wine vinegar
tt	sea salt
tt	black pepper, freshly ground

*remove from heat & let cool ~2-3 min
*add vinegar & scrape fond from pan bottom
*taste & adjust seasoning (should taste slightly acidic as the poached egg adds more fat to the dressing)

poach eggs
1 T	quality vinegar (mild flavor)

*fill a lg shallow pan with ~2" of water
*bring to a boil, then reduce heat to low to poach
*add vinegar to water

6	eggs

*crack one egg into a sm bowl
*gently slide egg into poaching water
*repeat with remaining eggs
*poach til egg whites turn white, ~3-5 min
*remove eggs with perforated spoon
*drain excess water – blot on paper towel

salad
1	lg head curly endive (aka frisee), cut in ~2" pieces, cleaned & spun dry (~8-10 c)
tt	sea salt
tt	black pepper, freshly ground

*place endive & croutons in lg bowl
*season greens lightly with S+P
*add dressing & poached eggs
*toss thoroughly
*taste & season further as needed
*serve immediately

We have made & served this dish every year to curious students & it is always met with resounding success. The flavors blend beautifully & the textures of soft pasta, crunchy pine nuts & creamy feta cheese are simply irresistible. This salad is a perfect winner for a party or picnic – but don't wait too long to get your own serving!

MEDITERRANEAN FREGOLA SALAD

(serves 8-10)

ingredients

pasta
2 c	fregola pasta
1 T	sea salt
1 T	extra virgin olive oil

vinaigrette
¼ c	red wine vinegar
1	shallot, minced
1	lemon, zested
2 T	lemon juice, freshly squeezed
1 t	smoky paprika
½ c	extra virgin olive oil
tt	sea salt
tt	black pepper, freshly ground

vegetables
2	sm zucchini or yellow squash, sliced into ½" planks
1-2 t	extra virgin olive oil

salad
½ c	pine nuts, toasted
1 c	feta cheese, crumbled
1 c	roasted red pepper, diced
¼-½	sm red onion, thinly sliced
⅓ c	kalamata olives, pitted & roughly chopped
8-10	fresh basil leaves, cut in a chiffonade
¼ c	fresh parsley leaves, minced

techniques

*bring a lg pot of water to a boil

*add fregola & salt to boiling water
*cook til fregola is al dente, ~12-15 min

*drain pasta, rinse with cold water & toss with oil

*put vinaigrette ingredients (except oil) in a sm bowl
*whisk to combine

*drizzle in oil while whisking constantly
*taste & adjust seasoning

*heat grill pan OR grill over med flame til hot
*brush vegetables with olive oil (both sides)
*grill vegetables til al dente, ~2-3 min / side
*remove from grill, cool & cut into ½" dice

*place fregola in a lg serving bowl
*add vegetables & remaining salad ingredients
*add a portion of vinaigrette to salad
*toss to coat, adding more vinaigrette as desired
*season with S+P
*let rest for ~30 min to combine flavors
*taste & adjust seasoning again as needed
*serve at room temp

chef notes

fregola is a toasted, sm round italian pasta that is not always easy to find (we sell it at the shop) – a good substitute is israeli couscous toasted in a dry pan ~2-3 min to achieve a golden color

ENTRÉES

I am frequently asked "what's your favorite dish?", to which I usually reply "that's like asking a parent to name their favorite child". That gets a good laugh, & then the crisis is averted. Truthfully, this IS one of the recipes I go to often...the flavors of salty, sour, sweet & bitter blend beautifully in this dish. Add garlic & red chili flakes & this is pretty close to food heaven! So, if I HAD to pick...

ORECCHIETTE PASTA WITH SAUSAGE & BROCCOLI RABE

(serves 4-6)

ingredients

1 T	sea salt

techniques
*bring a lg pot of water to a boil
*add salt to water

¼ c	extra virgin olive oil
1 lb	med spicy raw italian sausage (bulk) OR casings removed if links

*heat a lg heavy pot over med hi flame til hot
*add oil & swirl to coat
*add sausage
*break sausage up with a wooden spoon & cook til browned & cooked thru, ~7-10 min
*remove meat & drain in paper towel lined bowl

1 lb	orecchiette pasta

*start to cook pasta when meat is ~1/2 way done
*cook pasta using the pasta method
  (lg pot, boiling water, salt, cooked al dente)
*drain pasta (but do NOT rinse) & save ~1 c of pasta water

1	bunch broccoli rabe (~ 1 lb), dry ends removed & the bunch cut in ½" pieces crosswise

*add broccoli rabe to pot sausage was in
*cook til bright green & almost al dente, ~2-3 min

3	cloves garlic, minced
½-1 t	dried crushed red chili flakes

*add garlic & red chili flakes
*sauté til aromatic, ~1 min

¼ c	dry white wine

*add wine & cook ~1 min
*add meat back to pan
*add pasta & enough reserved cooking liquid, ~¼ c at a time, to moisten
*stir to incorporate
*remove from heat

1 c	finely grated parmesan cheese
tt	sea salt
tt	black pepper, freshly ground

*add cheese & stir to incorporate
*season to taste with S+P
*transfer to serving bowl(s)

6-8	basil leaves, cut in a chiffonade

*garnish with fresh basil

flavour favorites

This recipe is a real sleeper – with so few ingredients & steps, it might seem overly simplistic. Yes, it's simple, but the flavor you can achieve through braising elevates the final dish to utter scrumptiousness. We LOVE this chicken – it ranks amongst our favorites because it perfectly represents braising as a cooking technique. With just a few steps, the result is tender chicken, flavorful sauce, succulent & mellow softened garlic AND a sense of "wow...I just made that!".

40 CLOVE GARLIC CHICKEN
(serves 4-6)

ingredients

4-5 lb	whole bone-in chicken, cut into 8-10 serving pieces
tt	sea salt
tt	black pepper, freshly ground
1 T	grapeseed oil

40	cloves of garlic, whole & unpeeled
1 T	herbes de provence
1-2 c	chicken stock

techniques

*season chicken with S+P

*heat a lg heavy pot over med hi flame til hot
*add oil & swirl to coat
*add chicken, skin side down, & sear all sides til golden brown, ~6-8 min per side (sear in batches, if needed, to avoid overcrowding the pan)
*remove chicken & pour off excess fat from pan
*arrange chicken in one layer on pan bottom

*add garlic, herbs & stock (~½ way up meat)
*cover & braise on low heat til meat is falling from the bone tender (turn once ~½ way thru cooking), ~60-90 min total
*remove chicken
*increase heat to hi & reduce braising liquid to a sauce, ~7-10 min
*taste sauce & adjust seasoning
*serve chicken with softened garlic & sauce

chef notes

*this dish is best when using whole, bone-in chicken (even the breasts) – if the breasts are really large pieces, cut them in ½ thru the bone using a sharp chefs knife
*don't feel compelled to cut up your own chicken – most grocery stores carry cut up bone-in chicken
*DO feel free to peel all the garlic, as it will make eating the final dish easier – however this takes a bit of time...if you don't mind eating around the skins (they are very soft & the garlic slips out easily), just leave them on to cut your prep time down
*this dish can be braised in the oven too – try covered at 325° for ~60-90 minutes (flip once ~½ way thru)
*make sure that the meat is NOT simmering OR boiling during braising – it is important for the tenderness of the meat that it be on a very (very!) low simmer

Class regulars might recall my reticence for meatloaf...my mother made it every week when we were growing up (&, sorry mom, I'm afraid it was a rather uninteresting version at that!). THIS recipe usually garners comments from guests that it's what they WANT meatloaf to taste like! The mix of meats, the tasty bbq sauce on top & the inclusion of real, flavorful ingredients make THIS meatloaf a real family winner! ∽

HOMEMADE MEATLOAF

(makes one lg loaf, serves 6-8)

ingredients	techniques
	*preheat oven to 350°
	*line a sheet pan with parchment paper & set a wire cooling rack atop parchment
ketchup glaze	
1 c quality ketchup	*put all glaze ingredients into a sm saucepan
½ c packed dark brown sugar	*mix & set aside
½ c cider vinegar	
meatloaf	
2 T grapeseed oil	*heat a med skillet over med flame til hot
1 med onion, diced	*add oil & swirl to coat
	*add onion & sauté til softened, ~4-6 min
2 cloves garlic, minced	*add garlic & sauté til aromatic, ~30 sec
	*remove from heat & transfer to a lg bowl to cool
2 eggs	*put eggs, spices, mustard, worcestershire, tabasco & milk in a med bowl
½ t dried thyme	*whisk to combine thoroughly
1 t fine sea salt	
½ t black pepper, freshly ground	
2 t dijon mustard	
2 t worcestershire sauce	
¼ t tabasco OR chipotle tabasco	
½ c whole milk	
1 lb ground beef chuck	*put meats, panko & parsley into bowl with onion
½ lb ground pork	*add egg mixture to meats
½ lb ground veal	*mix thoroughly with fork OR hands til evenly blended & mixture does not stick to bowl (if sticking add a bit more milk)
2/3 c panko flakes	
1/3 c minced fresh parsley	*form meatloaf in one free-form loaf on the wire cooling rack set into the sheet pan
	*brush ~1/4 glaze over top of loaf
	*bake til glaze is set, ~40 min
	*brush with another ¼ of glaze
	*bake til loaf registers 160° internal temp, ~30-45 more min
	*remove & cool for at least 20 min
	*simmer remaining glaze over med low heat til thickened, ~10 min
	*slice loaf & serve with remaining glaze

At the onset of one of our amazing vacations, I ordered this pasta in venice. Then, I spent the reminder of our trip "chasing" this dish at other restaurants, only to feel each attempt fell a little short.. I certainly won't say any were bad (we were in italy, after all!). Returning home, it took me over five attempts to recreate it, which seems crazy as it has so few ingredients. The key is using an olive oil that is buttery & luscious AND making sure you season it with enough salt to pop the flavors. Enjoy the gratifying simplicity.

SPAGHETTI AGLIO E OLIO
(OLIVE OIL & GARLIC CHILI SPAGHETTI)
(serves 6-8 as an appetizer, 3-4 as a main course)

ingredients		techniques
1 T	sea salt	*bring a lg pot of water to a boil *add salt to water
1 lb	thick spaghetti noodles	*cook noodles using the pasta method (lg pot, boiling water, salt, cooked al dente) *start sauce when noodles are almost finished *drain noodles but do NOT rinse
½ c	extra virgin olive oil (see chef notes)	*heat a lg sauté pan OR lg soup pot over med flame til hot
4	cloves garlic, minced OR sliced	*add oil & swirl to coat
1½ t	dried crushed red chili flakes	*add garlic & red chili flakes *sauté til garlic is aromatic & tender, ~1 min *add cooked pasta & toss to coat thoroughly
tt	sea salt	*season pasta generously to taste

chef notes
*use a mild olive oil for this recipe (such as ranieri extra virgin) – we prefer something a bit more buttery & less flavorful...the quality & smoothness of the oil really make this dish
*don't be afraid of salting this dish – the flavors pop when enough salt is added
*consider garnishing with basil OR parsley (though we did not typically see this in our travels in italy)
*we did experience this once with a few shaved pieces of parmesan cheese – it was lovely this way

denise norton

flav

These wraps are easy, fresh, vibrant & irresistible! We've made these many times in kids classes & adult classes alike & they're always a favorite. The lettuce provides a crisp & refreshing package to the tasty, soft chicken & vegetables. Fun to make, fun to eat...need we say more?

CHICKEN LETTUCE WRAPS

(makes ~8 wraps)

ingredients		techniques
1	head iceberg, romaine OR bibb lettuce	*wash lettuce, dry & separate the leaves *set aside

sauce

¼ c	soy sauce	*mix sauce ingredients together in a sm bowl
¼ c	cold water	
2 T	oyster sauce	
2 T	rice wine vinegar	
1 T	cornstarch	
1 t	sugar	

stir fry

2 T	grapeseed OR peanut oil	*heat wok OR lg sauté pan over med hi flame til hot
1 t	sesame oil	*add grapeseed oil & swirl to coat
1 lb	ground chicken	*add sesame oil
		*add chicken & cook til chicken is just cooked thru, breaking meat with spoon, ~5-7 min
		*remove chicken from pan
1	red pepper, diced sm	*add red pepper & celery to pan
2	stalk celery, diced	*sauté til almost al dente, ~3-4 min
4	scallions, whites minced & greens sliced on a bias	*add scallion whites, garlic & ginger
2	cloves garlic, minced	*sauté til aromatic, ~30 sec
1 t	finely grated fresh ginger	*re-stir sauce & add to pan
		*bring sauce to a boil
		*add back chicken, stir, & heat thru
		*remove from heat
		*lay out lettuce leaves & add a spoonful of filling into the middle of each
		*garnish top with scallion greens
		*serve hot (eaten "taco" style)

This is our mise en place for this dish (everything in place). For many dishes, like this one, having all of your ingredients prepped, chopped & ready to go is important because the cook time is very short. Forget something & you might wind up overcooking your food while you finish prepping. For more on mise en place – see "recipes are a roadmap" in the front of the book.

This chili is featured in our pork 101 class. It requires a bit of work, especially when searing the meat, but it really showcases what you can do to tenderize a cheap, tough cut of pork. Once fully braised, the pork is succulent, the flavors are lightly spicy & well balanced & the kitchen smells outrageous! This is one of my all-time favorite recipes & pairs perfectly with a sunday afternoon, a beer & a bears football game!

SPICY PORK & RED BEAN CHILI

(serves 6-8)

<u>ingredients</u>

~2	ancho chilies, dry stems & seeds removed
3 c	boiling water

<u>techniques</u>

*put chilies in a sm heat proof bowl
*add boiling water & let sit to soften chilies, ~30 min
*purée chilies & water in a blender
*press mixture through a fine sieve
*discard any solid pieces & reserve chili liquid

½ lb	bacon, cut into ½" pieces

*put bacon in a cold, lg heavy soup pot
*cook over med hi heat til crispy, stirring often
*remove bacon, drain & reserve
*pour off all but ~1 T of bacon fat from pot

1 T	grapeseed oil
4 lbs	pork shoulder, bone out, fat trimmed & cut in ~½-1" cubes (aka pork "butt")
tt	sea salt
tt	black pepper, freshly ground

*add grapeseed oil to same pot & heat til hot
*season pork with S+P
*add pork to pan in ~4 batches (one layer)
*sear each batch to brown pieces on two sides, ~3-4 min per side
*remove each batch of pork from pot & reserve
*pour off all but ~1 T of fat & reduce heat to med

1	lg onion, diced

*add onion & sauté til tender, ~4-6 min

1	med jalapeno, seeded & diced sm
4	cloves garlic, minced

*add jalapeno & garlic
*sauté til aromatic, ~1 min

2 c	beef stock
1 c	brewed coffee
1	28 oz can crushed tomatoes
1 T	ground cumin
2 t	dried oregano
¼ t	cayenne pepper

*add stock, coffee, tomatoes & spices
*add ancho chili liquid
*return pork to pot with accumulated juices
*bring to a boil & reduce heat to low
*simmer (barely) til pork is tender, ~ 2-3 hrs, stirring occasionally

2	15 oz cans of red OR kidney beans, drained & rinsed
½ - 1	lime, juiced
tt	sea salt
tt	black pepper, freshly ground

*stir in beans & reserved bacon & heat thru
*add lime to taste
*taste & adjust seasoning
*garnish!

<u>suggested garnishes</u>
diced red onions, torn fresh cilantro, diced avocado, sour cream OR corn chips

flavour favorites

denise norton

101

Many (many!) years ago, a friend chatted up the "fish tacos" served at a restaurant near his home. I didn't get it. Fish on tacos? Really? I avoided them for a long time & then we scheduled a cooking class with fish tacos on the menu. I was sold after the first bite! This tasty recipe has a plethora of flavors & textures & every time we make them, we convert a few more people!

WHITEFISH TACOS WITH MANGO SALSA

(serves 4-6)

ingredients

salsa

2	sm ripe mangos, peeled & cut in 1-2" chunks
1	ripe avocado, cut in lg pieces
½	med red onion, cut in lg chunks
1-2	limes, freshly squeezed
2 T	vegetable oil
1-2 t	sambal
¼ c	fresh cilantro leaves
tt	sea salt
tt	black pepper, freshly ground

fish

4-6	tilapia OR other whitefish fillets, skinless & deboned
tt	sea salt
tt	black pepper, freshly ground
½ c	yellow cornmeal (fine ground)
4-6 T	vegetable oil

assemble dish

4-12	corn OR flour tortillas, warmed in oven
1	romaine heart, cleaned, julienned & spun dry
1	lime, cut into wedges

techniques

*put all salsa ingredients in a food processor
*pulse to create a salsa consistency (scrape as needed)
*taste & adjust seasoning & acidity
*let sit to blend flavors, ~15 min

*season fish with S+P
*place cornmeal in a shallow bowl
*dredge both sides of fish with cornmeal
*shake off excess cornmeal

*heat a lg sauté pan over med hi flame til hot
*add enough oil to create ~1/8" layer
*add fish carefully (may need to do in batches), fleshy side (presentation side) down first
*cook til golden & cooked thru, ~3-5 min per side
*remove to platter lined with paper towels
*keep warm

*place tortilla on serving plate
*top with fish (consider cutting fish into pieces if making 2 tacos per person)
*top with salsa & romaine
*garnish with lime wedge

chef notes

*to create the salsa without a food processor, cut the mango, avocado & onion into sm 1/8" pieces & mince the cilantro finely – stir all ingredients together
*one of our testers suggested diced tomatoes as an added garnish – we LOVE that idea!

The name is a misnomer – this is NOT my grandmother's pot roast recipe. Rather, it's what I WISH my grandmother's pot roast would have been! Sunday family suppers growing up often featured pot roast, but the meat was actually roasted in the oven & came out dry & stringy. The best pot roasts should be braised, allowing the tough meat to slowly break down & become fork-tender. Make sure you reserve the time to let it slow cook away until it's deliciously tender.

GRANDMA'S POT ROAST
(serves 4-6)

ingredients		techniques
3-4 lbs	boneless beef chuck OR rump roast, 2-3" thick	*let roast rest at room temp ~30 min
1 t	fine sea salt	*season roast with S+P on all sides
½ t	black pepper	*coat all sides with flour & shake off excess
2-4 T	all purpose flour	
3-4 T	grapeseed oil	*heat a lg heavy pot over med hi flame til hot
		*add oil & swirl to coat
		*sear roast on all sides til dark brown crust forms, ~6-8 min per side
		*remove meat from pot
		*remove all but ~1 T of fat from pot
1	medium onion, sliced	*add onions & carrots to pot
1	carrot, peeled & cut into coins	*sauté til aromatic, ~1-2 min
1 c	canned crushed tomatoes	*add tomatoes & heat through
		*add roast back to pot
1-2 c	beef stock	*add stock so liquid reaches ~½ way up meat
2 T	red wine vinegar	*add vinegar, thyme & tabasco to liquid
2 t	dried thyme	*reduce heat to low & cover
1 t	tabasco	*turn meat over once during braising ~½ way thru
		*braise til fork tender, 3–3½ hrs
		*add additional beef stock, as needed, while braising
		*remove roast from pot, remove external fat from meat & slice
		*reduce liquid, as needed, to thicken sauce to desired consistency
		*taste sauce & adjust seasoning
		*strain sauce & serve over pot roast

 chef notes

*make sure that the meat is NOT simmering OR boiling during braising – it is important for the tenderness of the meat that it be on a very (very!) low simmer
*chef ginna prefers NOT to strain the sauce after removing the meat but rather to puree the whole mixture to create a thicker sauce more like gravy (either final result is pretty tasty!)

This dish is usually met with surprise & delight! It's great for a family meal – interesting flavors for the adults, yet not spicy for the kids (only the poblano provide a small amount of heat). As one taste tester put it..."perfecto"!

MEXICAN GREEN CHILI WITH MEATBALLS

(serves 6-8)

ingredients

roast vegetables

1 lb	sm-med tomatillos, husked & washed
1	med white onion, peeled & cut in ½" chunks
4	cloves garlic, peeled
2	poblano chilies, stems & seeds removed, cut into 1" chunks

2 t	ground cumin
2 t	dried oregano

meatballs

1 lb	ground pork
½ c	uncooked long grain rice
1 T	chili powder
2 t	ground cumin
1 t	dried oregano
1 t	fine sea salt
½ t	garlic powder
2	eggs, beaten

chili

¼ c	vegetable oil
¼ c	masa harina (OR flour)

4 c	chicken stock

1 c	frozen corn
1-2 T	lime juice, freshly squeezed
tt	sea salt
tt	black pepper, freshly ground

some	sour cream
½ c	fresh cilantro leaves, roughly chopped

techniques

*preheat oven to 400°
*line 2 sheet pans with parchment paper

*put tomatillos, onion, garlic & chilies on one sheet pan
*roast in the oven til slightly charred, ~20-25 min

*transfer vegetables to a food processor
*add spices & pulse til mixture is chunky (like salsa)

*put pork in a med bowl
*sprinkle remaining ingredients over meat
*mix well with fingers to thoroughly combine
*shape into balls ~walnut size (~1 T) (try using a cookie scoop)
*place on 2nd sheet pan & set aside

*heat a lg soup pot over med hi flame til hot
*add oil & swirl to coat
*add masa, whisk to combine, & cook ~1-2 min

*add stock slowly, whisking after each addition
*add vegetable mixture to pot & stir thru
*bring to a boil, then reduce heat to low
*add meatballs carefully (they should be submerged)
*cover & simmer til rice is tender, ~30-40 min

*add corn & lime juice & heat thru, ~2 min
*taste & adjust seasoning & balance

*ladle chili into serving bowls
*garnish with sour cream & cilantro

f chef notes

*to add more kick & heat to this recipe, consider adding a whole jalapeno pepper (cut in ½ & seeded) to the vegetables to be roasted
*for garnishing, also consider ripe avocados, grated cheddar cheese & red onion

Our students are often looking for new inspiration to cook salmon. This recipe has quickly become a favorite – it's fast, flavorful & gorgeous! To save even more time, you can use a prepared bbq sauce, but please make sure to check the ingredient list to ensure it contains quality components (& not a lot of preservatives OR high fructose corn syrup). This one is a show-stopper!

GRILLED SALMON WITH SMOKY ESPRESSO BBQ SAUCE
(serves 4-6)

ingredients

bbq sauce

1 c	quality ketchup
½ c	balsamic vinegar
½ c	honey
¼ c	soy sauce
1 T	instant espresso granules OR powder
1 t	smoky paprika

1 T	extra virgin olive oil
2	cloves garlic, minced

salmon

4	4-6 oz salmon fillets OR 1 lg salmon fillet, ~1½ lb, skin on, scaled & deboned
tt	sea salt
tt	black pepper, freshly ground

techniques

*put ketchup, vinegar, honey, soy, espresso & paprika in a med bowl
*whisk to combine

*heat a sm sauce pan over med flame til hot
*add oil & swirl to coat
*saute garlic til aromatic, ~30 sec – 1 min
*add ketchup mixture to pan
*simmer to blend flavors & thicken sauce, stirring occasionally, ~15-20 min

*bring fish to room temp while heating grill & simmering sauce
*preheat grill – grates should be VERY hot
*clean grates to remove debris
*oil grates lightly, as necessary
*season salmon lightly with S+P
*place fish on hot grates, flesh side down
*leave grill lid open
*sear on 1st side til marks form, ~3-4 min
*flip
*brush flesh side with bbq sauce
*grill til almost cooked thru, ~3-4 more min
*remove fish from the grill
*brush with more sauce as desired
*let rest for ~5-7 min & serve hot

flavour favorites

Making vindaloo paste from scratch is not hard, it just takes a bit of time. The gorgeous fresh flavorings paired with good quality dried spices results in an incredibly full flavored vindaloo, which beats take out every time! Vindaloo DOES mean a bit of kick from chilies, but we find that you get flavor first, then a nice dose of heat with this paste. If you're a bit spice-shy, read the chef notes to learn more about how to control the heat level.

VINDALOO PASTE
(makes ~1/2 c)

ingredients

1 t	cumin seeds
1 t	mustard seeds
1 t	coriander seeds
4-6	sm dried red chilies, stems removed, minced (see chef notes)
4	cloves garlic, pressed
1-2	fresh red OR green chilies, seeded & finely diced (see chef notes)
¼ c	fresh cilantro leaves, minced
1 T	finely grated fresh ginger
1 T	turmeric
1½ t	garam masala
1 t	cayenne pepper
1 t	paprika
1 t	ground fenugreek
1 t	fine sea salt
3 T	peanut oil
2 T	tomato paste

techniques

*heat a sm sauté pan over med flame til hot
*add seeds & toast til aromatic, ~1-2 min
*place seeds in a mortar & pestle

*add dried chilies to mortar & pestle
*crush til mixture is well ground
*alternatively, use a spice grinder OR a mini food processor to grind spices
*place spice mixture in a med bowl

*add remaining ingredients to bowl
*stir thoroughly to combine

f chef notes

*this paste can vary widely in spiciness; for less heat, seed the dry chilies & use milder fresh red OR green chilies & for more heat, retain the seeds in the dry chilies & use fresh chilies that have more kick
*mild to medium heat fresh chilies = anaheim, fresno, hatch OR jalapeno
*medium to hot fresh chilies = jalapeno, chili de arbol, tabasco OR cayenne
*in our classes, we often have a pretty lively discussion about chilies...the heat in chilies can be quite variable, so we generally recommend that you cut them small & then "take one for the team" & taste...then feel free to vary how much you use depending upon your heat tolerance

The specific selection of spices for different curries is a matter of cultural tradition & can vary widely depending upon regional OR family preferences. What makes curry delicious, though, is the complex combination of spices & herbs, usually including chilies. Traditionally, spices are used both whole & ground, they are often toasted & can be added at different times during the cooking process to achieve different flavors in the dish. Make sure your spices aren't too old, though, or they won't add enough flavor in the curry to be noticed!

We've put our "go-to" recipes in this book, & I felt it wouldn't be complete without one curry recipe. So many people are scared of curries, as they think of them as simply that yellow stuff that comes out of a bottle. Truth is, there are so many types of curry across several cuisines & their flavor comes from a blend of fresh spices & other tasty flavorings like garlic, ginger & herbs. Vindaloo is an extremely flavorful & approachable indian curry & a great place to start your very own at-home curry adventure!

CHICKEN VINDALOO
(serves 4-6)

ingredients		techniques
4-6	chicken leg/thigh combos OR 1 whole bone-in chicken, cut into serving pieces	*let meat rest at room temp for ~30 min
¼ c	peanut oil	*heat a lg heavy pot over med hi flame til hot
tt	sea salt	*add oil & swirl to coat
tt	black pepper, freshly ground	*season chicken with S+P
		*add chicken, skin side down, & sear all sides til golden brown, ~6-8 min per side
		*remove chicken from pot
		*pour off excess fat from pan, leaving ~2 T
2	lg onions, sliced	*add onions to pot & toss to coat in fat
		*sauté til lightly browned & tender, ~6-8 min
2	cloves garlic, minced	*add garlic, ginger & vindaloo paste to pot
1 T	finely grated fresh ginger	*stir thru
1	recipe vindaloo paste (previous page)	*sauté til aromatic, ~30-60 sec
2	med tomatoes, seeded & diced	*add tomatoes & stir thru
		*add meat back to pot with accumulated juices
¼ c	apple cider vinegar	*add vinegar, sugar & water (so liquid reaches ~½ way up meat)
1 T	sugar	*bring to a boil
~2 c	water	*reduce heat to low, cover & braise ~30 min
		*remove lid & turn chicken over
		*raise heat slightly to a low simmer
		*cook, uncovered, stirring occasionally & allowing liquid to reduce to create sauce, til chicken is cooked thru & very tender, ~30-45 more min
		*taste sauce & adjust seasoning

chef notes
serve with cooked basmati rice, a warmed piece of naan & a dollop of quality greek yogurt on top!

Diplomacy is an important concept with rib-lovers…alas I would never step on anyone's toes regarding the BEST way to make & serve ribs! Let me just say that this recipe provides a scrumptious & relatively uncomplicated way to try for yourself if you're a bit intimidated. We first start with a flavorful wet cooking method (poach) to tenderize the ribs. Then, it's a homemade bbq sauce, a basting brush & a grill to achieve the sticky, finger-licking, tasty, caramelized exterior. Y-U-M!

SPICY HONEY CAJUN RIBS WITH HOMEMADE BBQ SAUCE

(serves 4-6)

ingredients

poach ribs
2	slabs baby back pork ribs
an	cold water

¼ c	soy sauce
1 t	black peppercorns
3	bay leaves
4	cloves garlic, peeled & roughly chopped
4	stems of fresh parsley
2 T	cajun spice blend

bbq sauce
1 c	quality ketchup
½ c	white wine OR cider vinegar
½ c	honey
½ c	dark brown sugar
¼ c	dijon mustard
1	lemon, freshly squeezed
¼ c	tabasco or other hot sauce
4 T	unsalted butter
4	cloves garlic, minced
1 T	fine sea salt
1 t	dried crushed red chili flakes
1 t	black pepper, freshly ground

grill ribs
2	slabs poached baby back pork ribs (see above)

techniques

*cut each slab of ribs in half between bones
*place ribs in a lg heavy pot
*add enough water to cover ribs as needed

*add soy, peppercorns, bay, garlic, parsley & spice to pot
*bring liquid to a boil
*reduce heat to low (poach)
*poach on low til ribs are knife tender, ~60-90 min
*remove ribs & discard liquid

*combine all sauce ingredients in a med saucepan
*bring to a boil over med heat
*reduce heat to low
*simmer til sauce has thickened & flavors have blended, ~30-45 min
*divide sauce into 2 bowls

*heat grill OR grill pan over med hi flame til hot
*brush ribs with portion of bbq sauce from one bowl
*grill ribs, basting with sauce, til ribs are sticky, caramelized & heated thru, ~2-3 min per side
*cut slabs into individual ribs
*serve with extra sauce for dipping from 2nd bowl

We've done many classes over the years on stir fry & its variations. This is a tasty basic recipe & can provide a strong foundation for your own deviations after you've practiced a time or two. If you're interested in adding meat, cook it in the pan before the veggies, remove it, then add the meat back into the stir fry after the veggies are done just to warm it thru (this way you don't over cook the meat). Any way you make it, we think it's way better than take-out!

ASIAN VEGETABLE STIR FRY WITH CILANTRO LIME RICE

(serves 4)

ingredients

rice
1 c	sushi rice
1¼ c	water (see pkg for proper hydration)

2-3 T	lime juice, freshly squeezed
¼ c	fresh cilantro leaves, roughly chopped
tt	sea salt

sauce
¾ c	chicken OR vegetable stock at room temp
2 T	soy sauce
2 T	water
2 T	cornstarch
1 T	sugar
1 T	mirin
1 t	sambal (optional & heat dependant)

stir fry
1 T	peanut OR vegetable oil
6 c	assorted vegetables, cut in bite-size pieces (zucchini, red pepper, celery, red onion, bean sprouts, asparagus, snow peas, carrots, scallions, broccoli, etc.)
1	clove garlic, minced

techniques

*place rice & water in heavy saucepan with a lid
*bring to a boil uncovered
*cover immediately & reduce heat to low
*cook til water has absorbed & rice is tender, ~15-20 min
*fluff with rice paddle or fork
*transfer to serving dish

*add juice, cilantro & salt to rice
*stir to incorporate
*taste & adjust seasoning & balance

*combine all sauce ingredients in a sm bowl

*heat a lg sauté pan OR wok over hi flame til hot
*add oil & swirl to coat
*add vegetables
*sauté til almost al dente, ~3-5 min

*add garlic & saute til aromatic, ~30 sec
*re-stir sauce to ensure it's well combined
*add sauce mixture & bring to a full boil
*remove from heat & serve over rice

f chef notes
this recipe creates a light amount sauce for the stir fried vegetables – if you prefer more sauce, consider doubling the sauce component

We make this salad in our kitchen skills class as a way to bolster confidence in some of our newer cooks. The techniques are straightforward & uncomplicated, but even so, the resulting dish is tasty & bright. This is one of those terrific recipes that doesn't take too long, creates a satisfying meal & looks pretty to boot!

GRILLED BALSAMIC BEEF & CUCUMBER SALAD

(serves 4-6)

ingredients

steak

~2 lbs	flank steak OR new york strip steak
1 T	balsamic vinegar
2 T	grapeseed oil
1 T	whole black peppercorns, crushed coarsely
tt	sea salt

salad

4-6 c	baby arugula OR spinach
1	english cucumber
2	carrots, peeled & grated
1-2 T	white wine OR balsamic vinegar
2 T	extra virgin olive oil
¼ c	fresh parsley leaves, roughly chopped
tt	sea salt

techniques

*brush both sides of steak with balsamic, then oil
*sprinkle with pepper
*let meat rest at room temp for ~30 min
*make salad while meat is resting

*heat grill OR grill pan over med hi flame til hot
*season both sides of steak with salt
*place steak on grill presentation side down
*grill steak til sear is created, ~5-7 min
*flip & grill til desired doneness
  (try a meat thermometer!)
*remove steak & put on a plate
*let rest ~5-10 min

*place arugula in a lg mixing bowl
*cut cucumber in ½ lengthwise & thinly slice
*add cucumber & carrots to arugula

*drizzle remaining ingredients over salad
*toss salad to coat
*let stand ~20 min at room temp to blend flavors
*taste & adjust seasoning prior to serving
*to serve, arrange salad on a lg platter
*cut steak against the grain into ¼" slices
*arrange steak atop greens
*serve warm

f chef notes

*in class, we generally cook the steak to ~135° internal temperature which is about medium (to try to satisfy a multitude of palates)
*as the meat rests, it will cook a bit more, so take that into consideration when deciding what temperature to pull it off the grill

These words come from our at-home recipe tester & frankly, we couldn't have scripted an intro better ourselves: "This is a very easy recipe that yields a dramatic & delicious outcome. There is a calming zen to the preparation: the methodic crosshatching, the placing of the roast on the bed of herbs; the filling of the slashes with the garlic, rosemary, & thyme; the salting & peppering; the saging...all were all enjoyable & rewarding. It looked gorgeous going into the oven, & even better coming out! The meat was tender & succulent. The exterior had the perfect texture – a decided crust without being dry. The herbs & garlic melded wonderfully with the pork, giving a balanced & complete profile." Wow...we're so proud!

TUSCAN GARLIC & ROSEMARY SLOW ROASTED PORK SHOULDER

(serves 6-8)

ingredients		techniques
		*preheat oven to 300°
1	head of garlic	*cut root off end of garlic
1	pkg fresh rosemary (15-20 sprigs)	*smash garlic cloves gently to remove the skins
		*smash garlic lightly again to break cloves into smaller pieces
		*put ~½ of garlic cloves & ~½ of rosemary sprigs into an oven proof pot with high sides
4-5 lbs	pork shoulder, bone in (if possible) (aka pork "butt")	*slash top & sides of meat in a crosshatch pattern with a sharp knife (~ ½-1" thick)
2 T	extra virgin olive oil	*place meat into pot atop rosemary & garlic (fat side up)
tt	sea salt	*drizzle lightly with oil & rub to coat meat evenly
tt	black pepper, freshly ground	*season with S+P generously
6-8	fresh thyme sprigs	*press remaining garlic into slits on top & sides
4-6	fresh sage leaves, minced	*break remaining rosemary up into smaller pieces & tuck rosemary & thyme into slits
		*sprinkle sage over top of pork
		*cover pot with lid (OR aluminum foil)
		*place pot into oven
		*roast til meat is tender easily falls apart, ~4-5 hrs, basting occasionally
		*remove from oven
		*transfer meat to a cutting board
		*break apart meat into serving hunks
		*season lightly with salt, as desired
		*serve hot

 chef notes

the pork for this recipe can be either bone in OR bone out – the addition of the bone will add flavor to the overall dish but will take slightly longer to cook

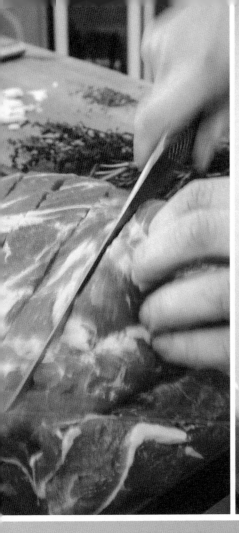

Risotto is a favorite dish for us to showcase in our classes – it's so incredibly versatile. While it might be considered a bit time-consuming, it's absolutely NOT hard to make. I always like to mention when I'm teaching that risotto is a GREAT dish to cook when you have guests in the kitchen – isn't everyone always asking what they can do to help you?! When they do, appoint them risotto stirrers (just make sure that you're the final taste tester!).

LEMON SPINACH RISOTTO WITH SHRIMP

(serves 4-6)

ingredients		techniques
2 T	unsalted butter OR extra virgin olive oil	*heat a lg heavy pan over med flame til hot
1	med onion, diced	*add butter & heat to melt
		*add onion & sauté til translucent, ~4-6 min
2	cloves garlic, minced	*add garlic & sauté til aromatic, ~30 sec
1½ c	arborio rice	*add rice & sauté til it turns white, ~ 1 min
½ c	dry white wine	*add wine & stir til liquid evaporates
4-5 c	chicken OR vegetable stock, heated	*add stock ~½ c at a time, stirring constantly
		*add next ladleful only after previous one has completely absorbed into rice
		*continue til rice is softened, ~20-24 min
4 c	baby spinach	*add spinach & stir thru
		*cook til partly wilted, ~2-3 min
1 lb	raw shrimp, peeled & deveined	*season shrimp lightly with S+P
tt	sea salt	*add shrimp & stir thru
tt	black pepper, freshly ground	*cook, stirring occasionally, til shrimp is opaque & cooked thru, ~3-4 min
1 c	finely grated parmesan cheese	*add cheese & lemon zest
1	lemon, finely zested	*stir & heat thru
tt	sea salt	*taste & adjust seasoning
tt	black pepper, freshly ground	*portion risotto into serving dish(es)
2 T	minced fresh chives	*garnish with chives

chef notes

we prefer to use smaller shrimp in this recipe (like 41/50's or 51/60's) so that they are relatively bite-size for the eater – if you choose a larger size, you may need to cook the shrimp a bit longer

flavour favorites

flavour favorites

I was adamant about including this recipe in the cookbook...but let me tell you it has created quite the controversy! Our tester found it too spicy, but after we got her to bring in some that she froze, we ate it & found it to be perfect. The moral of this story is that this chili is not for the faint of heart. It's not UBER spicy, but it's no wall-flower either. Go forth...make, eat & discuss!

BLOODY MARY CHILI
(serves 6-8)

ingredients		techniques
¼ lb	bacon, sliced in 1" pieces	*put bacon in a lg soup pot *heat over med flame *cook til crisp & browned, ~8-10 min, stirring often *remove bacon from pan, drain & set aside *leave ~2 T of bacon fat in pan, reserving any extra fat for 2nd batch of searing, if needed
1½ lbs	beef chuck roast, cut in ½" cubes	*season beef with S+P
tt	sea salt	*sear beef in batches (1st side, ~4-6 min, 2nd side ~3-4 min), adding more bacon fat as needed
tt	black pepper, freshly ground	*remove beef from pot & set aside
1	lg onion, diced	*add onion, pepper & celery to pot
1	green pepper, diced	*sauté til partly tender, ~4 min
3	stalks celery, diced	
2	cloves garlic, minced	*add garlic & jalapeno & spices
½-1	jalapeno, seeded & minced	*sauté til aromatic, ~1 min
2 T	chili powder	*return beef to pot
2 t	ground cumin	
1 t	dry mustard	
1 t	dried oregano	
½ t	cayenne pepper	
3 c	beef stock	*add stock, tomatoes & tabasco
1	28 oz can crushed tomatoes	*bring to a boil & reduce heat to low
½-1 t	tabasco sauce	*cover & braise til meat is tender, ~2– 2½ hrs
2-3 T	prepared horseradish	*remove from heat
1 T	worcestershire sauce	*add horseradish, worcestershire & lemon juice
1-2 T	lemon juice, freshly squeezed	*add celery salt
1 t	celery salt OR seeds	*stir thru
tt	sea salt	*taste & adjust seasoning
tt	black pepper, freshly ground	
some	celery ribs with leaves (to garnish)	*serve in bowls & garnish with celery & bacon

chef notes
other suggested garnishes include: sour cream, diced raw onion, pickled asparagus or other pickled veggies, green olives, pickled jalapenos & lemon wedges

We "discovered" this dish at a hole-in-the-wall restaurant in rome. Our cab driver at the vatican told us about his family restaurant & we just went with it. Happily, it did NOT disappoint. This recipe may not be entirely authentic (we couldn't quite translate everything from the obliging chef), but it comes close. Mangia, my friends, mangia!

SUMMER SQUASH PASTA WITH PANCETTA & PECORINO

(serves 4-6)

ingredients		techniques
1 T	sea salt	*bring a lg pot of water to a boil *add salt to water

8 oz	thick spaghetti OR linguine noodles	*cook noodles using the pasta method
		  (lg pot, boiling water, salt, cooked al dente)
		*drain pasta (but do NOT rinse) & save ~1 c of
		  pasta water

1 T 4 oz	extra virgin olive oil diced pancetta	*heat a lg pot over med flame til hot *add oil & swirl to coat *add pancetta & cook til crispy & cooked thru, ~6-8 min *remove pancetta & set aside
2 1 ½ 3	sm zucchini, julienned thinly sm yellow squash, julienned thinly sm red onion, thinly sliced cloves garlic, minced OR sliced	*add zucchini, squash, onion & garlic *toss with fat *cook til squash is just wilted, ~1-2 min *remove from heat *put pasta in pot with the squash
1 c 2 t 2 T	finely grated pecorino romano cheese finely grated lemon zest lemon juice, freshly squeezed	*add cheese, zest & lemon juice to pasta *toss mixture together *add some of the reserved pasta water if sauce becomes a bit sticky
~¼ t 1 T 10-12	black pepper, freshly ground minced fresh parsley leaves basil leaves, cut in a chiffonade	*season with pepper *add parsley & basil
tt tt some	sea salt black pepper, freshly ground extra virgin olive oil	*taste & adjust seasoning *drizzle a bit of oil over pasta, as desired *garnish with pancetta & more grated cheese, as desired

chef notes

*cut the squash into julienne pieces about the same width & length as the pasta – the aim in this recipe is for the cook time to be quick & the squash to be a substitute "noodle"
*we use (& sell!) a great tool called a julienne peeler to make the task of thinly slicing the squash quick & easy

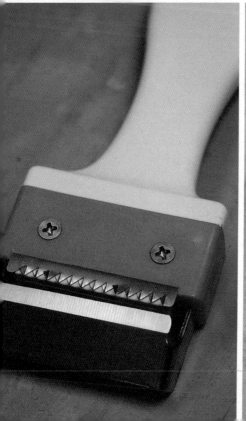

One might classify this recipe as a tad bit exotic, but it's really not. Think of it more as a glorified hamburger...instead of ground beef, it's lamb & instead of a bun, it's a pita. The quick salad that is tucked in with the meat makes it fresh & appetizing. I make this recipe often at home in the summertime. A glass of crisp white wine along with this dish on the deck...a heavenly greek meal, indeed!

LAMB KEFTA KEBABS
(serves 4-6)

ingredients

kebab
1½ lbs	ground lamb
¼ c	pine nuts
1	lemon, zested
2	cloves garlic, minced
2 T	fresh thyme leaves
1 T	ground cumin
1 T	chili powder
¾ t	fine sea salt
tt	black pepper, freshly ground

salad
4 c	baby arugula OR spinach
1	sm red onion, thinly sliced
½	english cucumber, grated
1 c	fresh parsley leaves, roughly chopped
¼ c	fresh mint leaves, roughly chopped
2-4 T	extra virgin olive oil
1-2 T	lemon juice, freshly squeezed
tt	sea salt
tt	black pepper, freshly ground

assemble
2-3	lg pitas OR flatbreads, cut in ½ & heated
½ c	quality plain greek yogurt

techniques
*preheat grill OR grill pan on med flame til hot

*place kebab ingredients into a lg bowl
*mix well to combine (do NOT overmix)
*divide mixture into 4-6 portions
*dampen hands lightly
*form meat into elongated sausage shapes
  (~4" long x 2" wide x 1" deep)
*grill kebabs til golden & just cooked thru,
  flipping once, ~8-10 min total
*let rest ~5-10 min

*put greens, onion, cucumber & herbs in a
  med bowl
*drizzle olive oil & lemon juice over salad
*toss to coat & season with S+P
*taste & adjust seasoning
*add more oil OR lemon juice as desired

*place pita on serving plate(s)
*portion salad over (OR into) pitas
*place kebabs atop salad (OR into) pitas
*add a heaping T of yogurt

flavour favorites

SIDE DISHES

A bowl of GOOD mashed potatoes is a culinary treasure! We teach MP often in classes & are always pleased when students pick up a pointer or two to make them taste better. Our most favorite tips to share…first, keep the potato pieces as large as you can (the smaller they are cut, the more water they take on, the more diluted the flavor). Second, start them in cold water so they cook more evenly. Third, use a ricer or a hand potato masher for mashing, not an electric mixer. The more the potatoes are worked, the starchier & gluier the texture can get. We've added a few ideas at the bottom of this recipe about how to flavor the potatoes to vary this side dish…the decision is now up to you!

MASHED POTATOES
(serves 6-8)

ingredients		techniques
3 lbs	yukon gold potatoes	*peel potatoes (OR scrub clean) & cut in equally-sized lg pieces (see chef notes)
1-2 T	sea salt	*place potatoes in a lg pot & cover with cold water
		*add salt & bring to a boil
		*reduce heat & simmer til knife tender, ~20-25 min
		*drain potatoes thoroughly
		*rice potatoes back into pot OR return potatoes to pot to mash by hand
4-6 T	unsalted butter, softened	*add butter & ~½ c of cream
1 c	heavy whipping cream, room temp	*mash with a hand potato masher OR stir thru if potatoes were riced
		*add more butter & cream a bit at a time & mash til desired consistency is reached
tt	sea salt	*taste & adjust seasoning
tt	black pepper, freshly ground	

chef notes
we strongly recommend keeping your potatoes as large as possible when you cook them (avoid the urge to quarter or dice them small as they take on water when they cook which can dilute their flavor) – do your best to cut them in very large like-sized pieces

try any of these great ways to create your own flavored mashed potatoes:

- *leeks, cut into matchsticks, & braised in wine & herbs ~30-40 min til tender*
- *horseradish*
- *roasted garlic (cut top ⅓rd off of head, drizzle with olive oil & roast til tender, ~45 min)*
- *truffle oil & chives*
- *caramelized onions*
- *bacon & cheddar*
- *wasabi (add water to dried wasabi powder to make a paste & let sit ~10 min)*
- *blue cheese*
- *fried pancetta & onion*
- *garlic grapeseed oil*
- *chipotle with adobo*
- *buttermilk & dill*

Colorful vegetables, a hint of zesty lemon & a smidge of char all add up to a delicious & healthy side dish! We prepare this recipe frequently in our classes as an accompaniment to a variety of main dishes – it's so versatile. We prefer the vegetables a bit al dente & really appreciate the pop of color they add to a plate.

CHAR ROASTED LEMON VEGETABLES

(serves 6-8)

ingredients	techniques
	*preheat oven to 450°
	*line a sheet pan with parchment paper (depending upon the size of the veggies, two sheet pans may be needed)
1 red pepper, julienned	*put vegetables on sheet pan
1 yellow OR orange pepper, julienned	
1 lb asparagus, dry ends trimmed & cut into 1" pieces	
1 lb sm-med brussels sprouts, ends trimmed & cut in ¼'s or ½'s (bite-size)	
1 sm red onion, julienned	
2-3 T extra virgin olive oil	*drizzle oil over vegetables
½ t dried thyme	*crumble thyme over vegetables
tt sea salt	*season lightly with S+P
tt black pepper, freshly ground	*toss to coat vegetables lightly with oil & seasonings
	*ensure vegetables are in one layer on pan
	*roast til vegetables are slightly charred & al dente tender, ~20-25 min
½ t finely grated lemon zest	*place vegetables in a serving bowl
2 T lemon juice, freshly squeezed	*sprinkle with zest & drizzle with lemon juice & oil
2 T extra virgin olive oil	*toss to coat
	*taste & adjust seasoning
	*serve hot

So...brussels sprouts...a food that often elicits disdain from many lovely folks. We're very proud to divulge that we've made numerous converts TO brussels sprouts with this exact recipe. The key, we've found, is the chiffonade (cutting the round sprout into thin ribbons so it's easier to eat). Oh, & adding wine. And, mustard. And pancetta!

SAUTÉED BRUSSELS SPROUTS WITH PANCETTA

(serves 6-8)

ingredients	techniques
1 lb brussels sprouts	*rinse brussels sprouts with cold water *pull off any limp outer leaves *trim tough ends off bottom of sprouts *cut each in half lengthwise *thinly slice brussels sprouts into 1/8" threads
4 oz diced pancetta (sm ~¼" cubes)	*put pancetta in a lg skillet *heat over med flame *sauté til crispy, stirring occasionally, ~8-10 min
2 T unsalted butter	*add butter to pan & heat to melt
2 sm shallots, diced 2 cloves garlic, minced	*add shallots & garlic to pan *sauté til aromatic, ~1 min *add brussels sprouts & stir to coat in fat *sauté til partially softened, ~3-5 min
¼ c dry white wine	*add wine & deglaze pan (scrape bits off bottom)
2 t whole grain OR dijon mustard	*add mustard & stir to combine *sauté til spouts are bright green & al dente, ~2-3 min more (do NOT overcook – they will be bitter & limp)
1-2 T lemon juice, freshly squeezed tt sea salt tt black pepper, freshly ground	*remove from heat *drizzle with lemon juice & season with S+P *taste & adjust seasoning

Here we show you with a picture how to achieve the thin ribbons, often called a chiffonade. This part of the prep takes a bit of time, however it can be done ahead & it makes the eating part a whole lot easier. We've even heard this dish being served at family dinners & the diners having no idea that they were eating brussels sprouts. Go figure!

Polenta is a wonderful side dish & a great alternative to mashed potatoes (not that there is anything wrong with mashed potatoes!). We have often commented in our classes that polenta recipes out there are frequently misguided – polenta needs flavor in the liquid that hydrates it to make it go from ordinary to extraordinary. Plain water simply won't do. Here, we use a combination of chicken stock & milk to cook the polenta to its velvety perfection. Check out the chef notes for some tasty variations to this basic recipe.

PARMESAN POLENTA

(serves 6-8)

ingredients		techniques
3 c	lightly flavored chicken stock	*put stock & milk in a med pot
1 c	whole milk	*bring to a boil
¼-½ t	fine sea salt	*add salt & reduce heat to a simmer
½ c	coarsely ground polenta	*combine polentas in a lg measuring cup with a spout
½ c	finely ground polenta	*stream polenta VERY slowly into liquid, stirring
		*reduce heat to low
		*cook til polenta thickens, comes away from sides of the pot, & tastes cooked, ~15-20 min, stirring often
2 T	unsalted butter	*add butter, cream & cheese
1/3 c	heavy whipping cream	*stir to incorporate
1 c	finely grated parmesan cheese	*too thick? add a bit more stock OR water too thin? heat a few min more
tt	sea salt	*taste & adjust seasoning
tt	black pepper, freshly ground	

chef notes

*if using a saltier chicken stock, consider adding less salt at the beginning & correcting the salt at the end of cooking

*if possible, use a combination of coarse & finely ground polenta for a better texture in your finished dish (one or the other can be used solely, however, the final consistency won't be as quite as interesting)

*we don't recommend instant polenta for this recipe as the flavor is not as complex

*a variety of other cheeses can be added to this recipe: blue cheese, goat cheese, sharp cheddar or even brie AND consider adding 1-2 T of minced fresh herbs at the end: chives, oregano, parsley OR thyme for a multitude of flavor options!

We understand that coleslaw is a very personal dish. Some people like it sweeter, some like it spicy, others prefer it more vinegary & yet others are purists about the ingredients. However you like it, this base recipe has genuine structure & you can vary it to your preference after it marinates for a while. If your penchant runs spicy, add ~½-1 t dried crushed red chili flakes to the dressing before you let it chill so the heat can permeate the dish. As for other preferences, adjust the flavor after the slaw has marinated...but don't forget to add salt so the flavors really blend!

BUTTERMILK COLESLAW

(makes ~10-12 c, serves 8-12)

ingredients

1	sm head of cabbage, cored & julienned in ~¼" x 2" pieces (~8 c)
½	lg onion, grated
4	carrots, peeled & grated
1	red pepper, cut in a ¼" dice

techniques
*place vegetables in a lg bowl

dressing

¾ c	buttermilk
½ c	quality mayonnaise
2 T	cider vinegar
2 t	celery seed
1t–1T	sugar
tt	sea salt
tt	black pepper, freshly ground

*put dressing ingredients in a med bowl
*whisk to combine
*add some of the dressing over vegetables & stir thru
*add more as desired
*chill at least 1 hr, ideally ~12 hrs
*taste & adjust seasoning & balance
  -too sweet? add more vinegar
  -too acidic? add a bit more sugar

6	scallions, sliced thinly on a bias
½ c	parsley leaves, roughly chopped

*remove salad from fridge ~30-60 min
  before serving
*add scallions & parsley to coleslaw
*stir thru

chef notes
*the amount of dressing increases the longer this chills (liquid emerges from the vegetables) – make sure to stir it well prior to final seasoning & serving to blend the flavors
*after the slaw has chilled in the fridge, taste it again & adjust it again to your liking using more sugar, acid OR mayo

Admittedly, this dish is a riff on a classic julia recipe. In hers, there is no cheese whatsoever, but the milk & butter make it FEEL ever so rich & creamy. We've adapted her timeless french recipe to add the gruyère, both for texture, color & (of course) even more deliciousness. Hats off to julia for the inspiration! Her indelible spirit lives on in our school's mission & in the hunger for learning our students bring to our table every day. Bon appetit! ✐◞

POTATO GRATIN WITH GRUYÈRE
(serves 6-8)

ingredients

techniques
*preheat oven to 425°

1 c	whole milk	
1	clove garlic, minced	
1 t	fine sea salt	
1/8 t	black pepper, freshly ground	

*put milk, garlic, S+P in a sm saucepan
*bring to a boil & turn off heat

8 oz   gruyère cheese, grated

*grate cheese & set aside

2 lbs   med-lg waxy red OR white potatoes

*peel potatoes & cut in ~1/8" thick slices
  (try a mandoline....carefully!)
*place ~1/2 of the potatoes evenly in an 11" ceramic
  pie dish, ~2" deep OR a 9 x 13" rectangular
  baking dish
*sprinkle ~1/2 of the cheese over the potatoes
*place remaining potatoes over cheese
*pour milk mixture carefully over potatoes

3-4 T   unsalted butter, cut in sm pieces

*distribute butter over the top
*sprinkle remaining gruyère over the top
*roast til milk is absorbed, potatoes are tender
  & top is golden brown, ~30-45 min
*remove from oven & let rest to set, ~15-30 min

🅕 chef notes
*the potatoes should be the last thing to mise en place – get everything else prepared, then peel & cut the
  potatoes so they don't oxidize (brown)
*resting allows the butter & any excess oils from the cheese to reabsorb into the potatoes which creates
  a better consistency for the gratin
*the gratin will be scoopable after ~15 min out of the oven & is sliceable after ~30 min

DESSERTS & SWEETS

This recipe came to us from a dear flavour friend & celebrated new york times bestselling author elizabeth berg. We tweaked it a bit & served them at one of her book signings at the shop (to RAVE reviews). Needless to say, we've been making them ever since! One of the best things about them is their simplicity – dry ingredients, wet ingredients, a bit of mixing & you get moist, complex, not-too-sweet, cupcake-store cupcakes!

CHOCOLATE CUPCAKES WITH CREAM CHEESE ICING
(makes ~2½ dozen cupcakes)

ingredients

techniques
*preheat oven to 350°
*line three standard muffin tins with paper liners

cupcakes
1¾ c	flour
2 c	sugar
¾ c	unsweetened cocoa powder, sifted
2 t	baking soda
1 t	baking powder
1 t	fine sea salt

*put dry ingredients in the bowl of a stand mixer
*whisk by hand to combine

1 c	strong brewed black coffee
1 c	buttermilk
½ c	vegetable oil
1 t	vanilla extract

*put wet ingredients (excluding eggs) in a med bowl
*whisk to combine
*add wet ingredients to stand mixer

2	eggs

*add eggs to stand mixer
*whisk at med speed 2 min (batter will be thin)
*divide mixture amongst muffin tins (fill ~½ full)
*bake til tester comes out clean, ~20-25 min
*cool in muffin tins on a wire rack
*remove cupcakes carefully from tins after ~15 min
*cool completely

icing
8 oz	neufchâtel cream cheese, softened
8 T	unsalted butter, softened
2 c	powdered sugar, sifted
1 t	vanilla bean paste OR extract
pinch	fine sea salt

*put icing ingredients in the bowl of a stand mixer (paddle)
*beat on low speed til incorporated
*increase speed to hi & beat til light & fluffy, ~5 min
*ice cool cupcakes with a spatula OR a piping bag

chef notes
*we prefer to transfer the finished batter from the stand mixer to a lg liquid measuring cup with a spout (at least 6 c capacity) & then use the measuring cup to fill the muffin liners
*don't be tempted to fill past ½ full as these cupcakes rise significantly & can tend to overflow & stick to the muffin pan (make a few extra cupcakes instead!)

This recipe has been a perennial favorite of kids & adults alike & often we hear "this is so easy & so delicious"! We also think it makes a poignant statement about cooking from scratch. Read the ingredients on a package for instant butterscotch pudding & you'll find a list of chemicals, several coloring agents & other unpronounceable additives. This pudding is the real deal...with only a few genuine ingredients, you can create a homemade dessert that is scrumptious & all natural!

BUTTERSCOTCH PUDDING
(serves 6-8)

ingredients		techniques
1/3 c	whole milk	*put milk, cornstarch, & salt in a sm bowl
¼ c	cornstarch	*whisk to combine (this is called a slurry)
1/8 t	fine sea salt	
8 T	unsalted butter	*put butter & sugar in a med saucepan
1 c	packed dark brown sugar	*heat over med flame
		*cook, whisking occasionally, til butter melts
1 c	heavy whipping cream	*add cream, milk & vanilla to pan
½ c	whole milk	*whisk to combine
2 t	vanilla bean paste OR extract	*remix slurry, add to pan & whisk to combine
		*whisk continuously til mixture thickens & boils in the middle of the pan, ~5 min
		*remove from heat
2	egg yolks	*whisk yolks into the mixture, one at a time
		*strain thru a fine mesh strainer into a clean bowl
		*cover with plastic wrap touching the pudding
		*chill at least 2 hrs
		*stir vigorously before serving

chef notes
consider topping with some unsweetened whipped cream for an extra flourish!
vanilla bean paste is a slightly more exotic ingredient that contains vanilla bean seeds which create a lovely, flecked appearance — it generally can be found at specialty food stores & measures the same as extract (so if you can't find it, just be sure to use REAL vanilla extract!)

This cake is for the lemon lover. Some of the comments from our taste-tasters include... "lemon-o-rama", "very bright, dramatic lemon flavor", & "cake is moist, curd pops, very bright"! There is a really nice balance of moist, delicate, sweet cake & lemony, creamy, brilliant curd that play so well together in this recipe. Lemon lovers, prepare to pucker up & enjoy!

PURE LEMON CAKE

(makes a 9x13 sheet cake OR one double layer 8 OR 9" round cake)

ingredients		techniques
1-2 T	unsalted butter	*preheat oven to 325°
1-2 T	flour	*butter & flour cake pan
		(either one 9x13x2 rectangular pan OR
		two 8 OR 9" round cake pans)
		*tap out excess flour
2½ c	flour	*put flour, baking powder & salt in a med bowl
2½ t	baking powder	*whisk til well combined
½ t	fine sea salt	
4	eggs	*put eggs & sugar in the bowl of a stand mixer
2 c	sugar	(whisk)
		*whisk on hi speed til light & fluffy, ~3-4 min
		(if using a hand mixer, whisk for 6-8 min)
1 c	vegetable oil	*put oil, zest & juice in a measuring cup
2	lemons, finely zested	with a spout
1 c	lemon juice, freshly squeezed	*reduce mixer speed to med
		*drizzle oil mixture gradually into egg mixture
		*turn off mixer
		*add dry ingredients to batter in 2 additions
		& mix each thru by hand til smooth
		*transfer batter to prepared pan(s)
		*bake til lightly golden, pulling away from sides
		& a toothpick inserted comes out clean,
		~50-60 min for sheet cake OR~30-35 min
		for round cakes
		*cool completely
1	recipe lemon curd (next page)	*unmold round cakes from pans
		*slather curd atop cake (sheet cake) OR divide
		curd to use between & atop cakes (round)

chef notes

*generally speaking, usually one lemon yields about 2-3 T of juice & just shy of ~1 T of zest
*it took ~6-8 lemons for the cake recipe in our testing & ~6-8 lemons for the curd (très lemony!)

Lemon curd is a pastry shop fundamental because it has so many uses: donut filling, crêpe topper, scone spread, or a lemon chantilly (by folding in some whipped cream). There is really nothing like making homemade lemon curd...it's tart, luscious, & absolutely irresistible. We've included this recipe as an indulgent topper to the pure lemon cake, but it certainly can stand on it's own for your next tea party!

LEMON CURD
(makes ~ 2 c)

<u>ingredients</u>

4	whole eggs
4	egg yolks
1 1/3 c	sugar
3 T	finely grated lemon zest
1 c	lemon juice, freshly squeezed
pinch	fine sea salt
8 T	unsalted butter, cubed

<u>techniques</u>

*put ingredients (except butter) into a
 med heavy saucepan
*whisk to combine & break up yolks

*add butter to saucepan
*cook over med low heat, whisking constantly
 til butter melts & curd thickens (don't boil),
 ~12-15 min
*strain thru a fine mesh strainer into a clean bowl
*cover with plastic wrap touching the curd
*refrigerate til cool, ~60-90 min

*re-whip curd with spoon OR whisk before using

chef notes
*be patient while stirring the curd – the mixture turns from a sloshy liquid to a "loose pudding" consistency pretty quickly as the egg cooks gently & coagulates...just when you think it's not working & you can't stir any more, it will thicken up on you!
*don't be tempted to turn up the heat too high on the curd because it can cook the eggs too quickly & cause them to curdle instead of gently thicken – the straining after cooking can catch some light curdling, but too much heat is not good for the curd

These little gems are potent, chocolate-y packages of pure decadence! Years ago, one of my talented chef instructors shared the recipe for these cookies & we've made them for countless classes & events to thundering applause! The sprinkle of salt mid-way through the baking process is really the pièce-de-résistance, taking them from ordinary chocolate cookies to extraordinary adult temptations. Try them with a glass of good port OR, of course, a tall glass of cold milk. We promise you'll thank us! ❧

CHOCOLATE FLEUR DE SEL COOKIES
(makes ~3-4 dozen cookies)

ingredients
16 T   unsalted butter, softened
1/3 c   packed dark brown sugar
1/3 c   sugar
1 t   vanilla extract

2 c   flour
½ c   cocoa powder (NOT dutch processed)
¼ t   fine sea salt

2 c   chocolate chips (semi OR bitter sweet)
2-3 T   milk

some   fleur de sel to garnish

techniques
*put butter, sugars & extract in the bowl of a stand mixer (paddle)
*cream til well combined, ~3-4 min

*put dry ingredients in a med bowl
*whisk (OR sift) to combine & break up lumps

*add ½ flour & ½ chips to butter mixture
*mix on low til almost combined
*drizzle milk over mixture
*add remaining flour & chips
*mix on low til just combined – do NOT overmix (dough will seem crumbly & a bit dry)
*separate dough into two batches
*shape dough into two ~1½" wide logs, pressing & gently squeezing to remove air pockets while shaping
*wrap in parchment paper & twist ends to seal
*refrigerate til hardened, ~1 hr

*preheat oven to 350º
*line 2 sheet pans with parchment paper
*cut cookies from log with serrated knife ~¼" thick
*place cookies on sheet pans
*bake cookies for 10 min til cracks start to form
*sprinkle a bit of fleur de sel on each cookie
*finish baking til set, another ~6-8 more min
*let cookies set on baking sheet ~5 min
*transfer from baking sheet to cooling rack
*cool (if you can resist!)

New girl in the condo building brings berry crisp to each of her five neighbors, mostly because she's gone to the farmers market & purchased about $25 of berries that she cannot possible eat herself! That was me, almost 15 years ago, & let me tell you that bringing berry crisp as a gesture of friendship is the right way to meet new neighbors! We've been teaching this recipe every year since the beginning of flavour. One of its biggest selling points is adaptability...it can be a summer farmer's market crisp with berries, or a fall dessert for the holiday season (think apples, pears & cranberries, oh my!).

FARMERS MARKET BERRY CRISP
(serves 6-8)

ingredients

topping
½ c	flour
¼ c	packed dark brown sugar
¼ c	sugar
½ t	ground cinnamon
¼ t	ground nutmeg
¼ t	fine sea salt
8 T	unsalted butter, cold, cut in sm pieces
1 c	quick oats

filling
6 c	mixed fresh berries, cleaned & cut in ~1" pieces
¼-½ c	sugar
3 T	cornstarch
1 T	finely grated lemon zest
2 T	lemon juice, freshly squeezed

techniques
*preheat oven to 350°
*lightly butter an 11" ceramic pie dish OR a 9" x 9" square baking dish

*put flour, sugars & spices in a food processor
*pulse several times to combine

*add butter & pulse til it is the size of sm peas

*add oats & pulse only a few times to combine
*place topping in fridge til ready to use

*put fruit in a lg bowl & add remaining ingredients
*toss fruit gently to coat
*transfer filling into baking dish in an even layer
*cover with an even layer of topping
*bake til filling is bubbly & top is golden, ~50-60 min
*serve warm OR at room temp

chef notes
*of course, this dish is amazing with some vanilla ice cream!
*taste the fruit to decide how much sugar to use – really tart fruit & berries will require the top end of the sugar range
*consider adding up to 1 c of lightly chopped nuts (pecans, walnuts OR hazelnuts) with the oats & pulse to chop a bit further & combine with the topping
*summer fruit combos: strawberries, blueberries, raspberries, blackberries, peaches, cherries
*winter fruit combos: apples, pears, cranberries, frozen OR dried cherries, frozen fruit (such as berries OR peaches OR mangos)

flavour favorites

FARMER'S MARKET BERRY CRISP

We've been cooking up peanut brittle every year for our village holiday walk, our anniversary party open house & our december hands-on cookie exchange classes. I know some folks can be a bit intimidated when it comes to working with sugar, but this recipe is pretty fool-proof. A clip-on thermometer is a key tool when it comes to making candy to achieve the right temperature & consistency. Every year, guests at the holiday walk remark about how the brittle is nicely crispy & crunchy, but it doesn't stick to your teeth. One year we didn't make brittle & boy, we heard about it!

PEANUT BRITTLE

(makes ~4 dozen sm pieces)

ingredients	techniques
1 T unsalted butter	*butter a sheet pan lightly
1½ c sugar	*put sugar, corn syrup, water & salt in a saucepan
¾ c lite corn syrup	*equip saucepan with a candy thermometer
½ c water	*heat over med hi flame til temp reaches 240°
½ t fine sea salt	(do NOT stir)
12 oz spanish peanuts	*add peanuts, stir & increase heat to hi
	*stir constantly & bring temp up to 295° AND mixture is golden/brown in color throughout (this can take the temp as high as ~320°)
1 T unsalted butter	*remove from heat
1 t vanilla bean paste OR extract	*add butter & vanilla & stir til butter melts
1½ t baking soda	*add baking soda (mixture foams up)
	*stir til combined
	*pour immediately onto prepared sheet pan
	*let settle in middle of pan (don't need to spread)
	*cool ~1 hr
	*break into bite-sized serving pieces

chef notes

*for a thinner brittle, carefully (as the sheet pan will get hot) tilt the pan side to side to stretch out the mixture
*we don't recommend spreading the mixture with a spatula as that can deflate some of the air bubbles created by the baking soda causing the brittle to be more dense & sticky
*don't be tempted to taste or touch the golden candy in the pot or on the pan til it cools off – the heated sugar can be in excess of 300° & can create some pretty serious burns (ask chef denise!)

You read the title correctly…this cake has rosemary in it! While the pungent herb might be an improbable flavoring for a dessert, this delightful, zesty, lemony cake is a perfect pairing for the rosemary. The flavor is lovely & tart, & it finishes with just a hint of herby indulgence. I recently served this at a dinner party & our charming british hostess clare exclaimed, "oh, I do so LOVE cake". This one is a dark horse, but continually emerges a winner!

LEMON ROSEMARY OLIVE OIL CAKE
(makes one 9-10" single layer cake)

ingredients
1 T	extra virgin olive oil
1 T	flour

3 c	flour
1 T	minced fresh rosemary
2 t	baking powder
½ t	baking soda
½ t	fine sea salt

3	eggs
1½ c	sugar
1 T	finely grated lemon zest
¼ c	lemon juice, freshly squeezed
½ c	extra virgin olive oil
½ c	whole milk

glaze (make right before icing cake)
2 c	powdered sugar, sifted
1 t	finely grated lemon zest
2-3 T	lemon juice, freshly squeezed

techniques
*preheat oven to 350°
*oil a 9 – 10" springform OR cake pan lightly
  (pan height should be at least 2" tall)
*line the bottom of pan with parchment paper
*oil over parchment paper & flour the pan
*tap out excess flour

*put flour, rosemary, baking powder, baking soda
  & salt in a med bowl
*whisk to combine dry ingredients

*place eggs → milk in the bowl of a stand
  mixer (paddle)
*beat on low speed til smooth, ~2-3 min
*add flour mixture
*mix on low speed til just blended – do NOT
  overmix
*transfer batter to prepared pan
*bake til toothpick OR cake tester comes out
  clean, ~35-45 min
*cool ~20 min in pan
*turn cake out onto wire rack
*place wire rack over a sheet pan (to catch drips)

*put powdered sugar & zest in a med bowl
*add juice a bit at a time & mix to incorporate
*too thick? add a bit more juice (sparingly)
*too thin? add more powdered sugar
*drizzle glaze immediately over warm cake

chef notes
*it takes ~3-4 whole lemons to make this cake & glaze

Here's the thing…making brownies from scratch is ALMOST as easy as using a box mix. The beauty…from scratch brownies means you're 100% sure of what's going into them & we are BIG fans of that! We made this recipe even more decadent by adding some gorgeous raspberries so you get a tart surprise in each brownie. Our guests love these which makes us want to share this recipe – the simplicity, the richness & the chocolate gooeyness.

FUDGY CHOCOLATE RASPBERRY BROWNIES

(makes 16 brownies)

ingredients		techniques
1 T	unsalted butter	*preheat oven to 350°
~2 T	flour	*butter & flour a 9" square springform OR brownie pan
		*tap out excess flour
1 c	semi-sweet chocolate chips OR quality chocolate, cut in sm pieces	*bring ~1-2" of water to a boil in a double boiler
¼ c	unsweetened chocolate chips OR quality chocolate, cut in sm pieces	*turn off heat
		*put chocolates & butter in top of double boiler in a clean dry bowl (do NOT let bowl touch water)
16 T	unsalted butter, cut into sm pieces	*let mixture melt, stirring occasionally
		*once smooth, remove from double boiler
		*cool mixture to lukewarm
2 c	packed dark brown sugar	*add sugar to chocolate mixture
		*mix well by hand
4	eggs	*whisk in eggs one at a time
1½ c	flour	*add flour, raspberries, vanilla & salt
1 c	fresh OR frozen raspberries, thawed	*mix til just combined
2 t	vanilla extract	*transfer to baking dish & spread batter evenly
1 t	fine sea salt	*bake til toothpick almost comes out clean, ~45-50 min
		*cool in pan ~45 min
		*slice & serve warm OR room temp

chef notes

we prefer to use a square springform pan for these – the sides can be removed once the brownies are baked so the brownies are easier to slice & remove from the pan

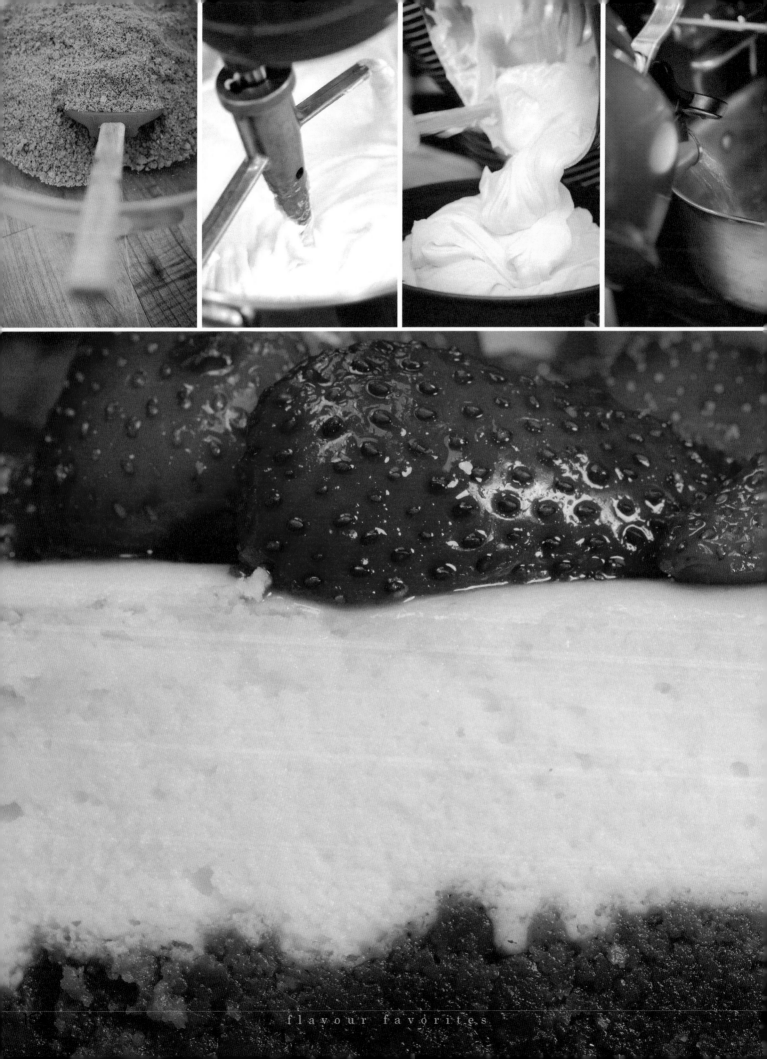

When we asked our customers to share what recipes they wanted to see in this book, we received multiple requests for this cheesecake. The mascarpone cheese in the batter provides a delightful tang, & students continually rave about the ease of preparation, yet the complexity & sophistication of the flavors. Buttery rich crust, tart cheese, sweet strawberries & pungent balsamic combine for an ultimate cheesecake experience!

MASCARPONE CHEESECAKE WITH BALSAMIC STRAWBERRIES

(makes one 9 OR 10" cheesecake)

ingredients	techniques
	*preheat oven to 350°
	*boil a teakettle full of water
	*place a leakproof 9-10"springform pan inside a lg roasting pan (note: if springform isn't leakproof, line the outside bottom & sides of pan with foil)

<u>crust</u>

10 oz dry almond cookies OR graham crackers	*place cookies in a resealable plastic bag
8-10 T unsalted butter, melted	*crush cookies into fine crumbs with meat mallet (alternatively, use a food processor)
	*put 2 c of crumbs into a med bowl
	*add butter as needed so crumbs hold together when squeezed (don't allow butter to ooze)
	*press crumbs firmly into bottom of springform pan & slightly up sides, if desired
	*chill while making filling

<u>filling</u>

2 lbs cream cheese, softened (four 8 oz pkgs)	*put cheeses & sugar in a lg bowl
1 c mascarpone cheese, softened	*beat with electric or stand mixer (paddle) til smooth, ~2-3 min, scraping sides
1¼ c sugar	
2 eggs	*add eggs, one at a time, & mix thru
	*spread mixture evenly over crust
	*place springform pan back into roasting pan
	*pour boiling water gently ~½ way up outside of springform to create a water bath
	*bake til cheesecake is lightly golden & quivers slightly as a whole (will also slightly pull away from the sides), ~70-90 min
	*remove springform carefully from roasting pan
	*cool to room temp ~1 hr & refrigerate ~2-3 hrs to set

<u>balsamic strawberries</u>

1 pt strawberries, hulled & quartered (~ 3 c)	*put strawberries, vinegar & sugar in a med bowl
¼ c balsamic vinegar	*stir gently to thoroughly combine
⅓ c sugar	*let stand at room temp til juices form, ~30 min
	*let cheesecake sit at room temp ~30 min
	*cut cheesecake into wedges & top with strawberries

These cookies are one of the newest additions to our favorites list, but boy have they drawn a legion of followers! The minute one says, "here, try a cookie with bacon in it", it certainly raises an eyebrow or two. I liken these tasty morsels to breakfast in a cookie (like pancakes, syrup & bacon all in one). You can bake them either chewy OR crispy... they're incredibly addictive, so don't say we didn't warn you!

MAPLE BROWN SUGAR BACON COOKIES

(makes ~5 dozen sm cookies)

ingredients

bacon

1 lb	bacon

cookie batter

3 c	flour
1 t	baking soda
1 t	fine sea salt
16 T	unsalted butter, softened
1 c	packed dark brown sugar
1 c	sugar
2 T	maple syrup
2	eggs

techniques

*preheat oven to 325°
*line two sheet pans with parchment paper
*cook bacon first & prepare batter while it cooks

*remove entire slab of bacon from pkg
*cut into ½" pieces
*place bacon in a med sauté pan
*heat over med hi flame
*cook, stirring often, til cooked thru & very crispy, ~15-20 min
*remove meat & drain in paper towel lined bowl
*cool slightly, then chop bacon into smaller pieces

*put dry ingredients in a med bowl
*whisk to thoroughly combine

*put butter, sugars & syrup in the bowl of a stand mixer (paddle)
*cream on hi speed til light & fluffy, ~2-3 min
*scrape down sides of bowl

*add eggs, one at a time, & mix thru
*add flour mixture in 3 batches, mixing on low (do NOT overmix)
*scrape down sides of bowl
*add in bacon
*stir with a wooden spoon by hand til bacon is mixed thru
*portion dough with cookie scoop (1 T) onto sheet pans (leave ~2" between as they spread)
*flatten slightly with hand or spoon
*bake til lightly golden, 12-15 min, rotating as needed for even cooking (oven dependant)
*cool on sheet pan ~5 min
*transfer to wire racks to cool
*repeat with remaining batter

chef notes

cookies DO continue to cook after they come out of the oven & while they are resting on the sheet pan...so, for slightly chewier cookies, bake for less time & for more crisp cookies, bake longer

denise norton

167

Yep…it's a fruit salad. BUT, it's a fruit salad with a twist! We've added a minted simple syrup with orange zest to the fruit, which provides an unusual, sweet enhancement to a traditional fruit bowl. Feel free to vary the fruit a bit. This makes a nice "dish to pass" at a picnic or family gathering. Don't forget to read the chef notes below about any leftovers (hint…sangria anyone?!).

MINTED ZESTY FRUIT SALAD WITH VANILLA

(serves 8-12)

ingredients

simple syrup
½ c	sugar
½ c	water
1	orange, zested & juiced
1 t	vanilla bean paste OR extract

12-14	fresh mint leaves, minced

salad
1 lb	strawberries, hulled & cut in bite-size pcs
1 pt	blueberries, cleaned, picked thru & de-stemmed
2 c	red grapes, cleaned & cut in ½ or ¼'s
2 c	green grapes, cleaned & cut in ½ or ¼'s
½-1	sm pineapple, outer portion removed, cored & cut into sm bite-size pieces (~3 c of cut pineapple)

techniques
*make simple syrup before cutting fruit

*put sugar, water, zest, juice & vanilla in a sm saucepan
*bring to a boil
*reduce heat to a simmer
*simmer to blend & thicken slightly, ~10-15 min
*turn off heat

*add mint leaves to simple syrup
*cool syrup to room temp while cleaning & cutting fruit

*put fruit in a lg serving bowl
*drizzle a portion syrup over salad
*toss thru – taste & add more syrup as desired

chef notes
*feel free to vary the fruit with other berries or bite-size pieces of apple, ripe peaches OR plums
*we have (very successfully!) frozen the leftovers of this salad, placed the frozen fruit in a pitcher, added some white wine & made a pseudo-sangria (& it was yummy!)

denise norton

These cinnamon rolls almost need no introduction! We serve them at all of our open house & customer appreciation events. We even have one customer who made them a LOT when she was expecting…we'd call THAT a flavour craving! ❧

QUICK BUTTERMILK CINNAMON ROLLS
(makes 8 lg rolls)

ingredients

8 T	unsalted butter, melted (for entire recipe)

filling

¾ c	packed dark brown sugar
¼ c	sugar
2 t	ground cinnamon
1/8 t	ground cloves
1/8 t	fine sea salt

dough

2½ c	flour
2 T	sugar
1¼ t	baking powder
½ t	baking soda
½ t	fine sea salt
1¼ c	buttermilk
1	recipe cinnamon roll icing (next page)

techniques

*preheat oven to 425°
*brush a 9" cake pan OR pie dish with ~1 T
 of the melted butter

*put filling ingredients in a med bowl
*add 1 T of the melted butter
*incorporate butter with clean fingers OR fork
 til mixture resembles wet sand
*set aside filling

*put dry dough ingredients in a separate med bowl
*whisk to thoroughly combine

*add buttermilk & 2 T of the melted butter to
 dry ingredients
*mix with a wooden spoon til liquid is absorbed,
 ~30 sec (dough will look "shaggy")
*transfer dough to a lightly floured work surface
*knead by hand til smooth/not shaggy, ~8-12 turns
*pat dough by hand into ~9"x12" rectangle
 ("landscape" on work surface)
*brush with ~2 T of the melted butter
*sprinkle evenly with filling, leaving ~½" border
*press filling lightly into dough
*roll into tight log, lengthwise (use bench scraper
 & lightly floured hands to help roll from top down
 OR bottom up)
*pinch seam tight & put seam side down
*cut log evenly into 8 pieces
*put 1 roll in the center of prepared pan
*surround with remaining rolls (around the edge)
*brush top with ~2 T of the melted butter
*bake til puffed & lightly golden, ~22-25 min
*cool ~8-10 min in pan

*make icing while rolls are cooling
*drizzle / spoon icing over rolls & serve warm

CINNAMON ROLL ICING

(ices 8 rolls)

<u>ingredients</u>		<u>techniques</u>
2 T	cream cheese, softened	*whisk together cream cheese & buttermilk
2 T	buttermilk	thoroughly (no lumps), ~1 min
1 c	powdered sugar	*sift powdered sugar over cream cheese
		*whisk til smooth glaze forms, ~30 sec
		*thin with buttermilk OR thicken with slightly
		more powdered sugar
¼ t	vanilla extract OR vanilla bean paste	*add vanilla & stir to incorporate

This dessert is stunning in a visual sense & lusciously sinful in a culinary sense! We've made this frozen mousse with a variety of other ingredients, including raspberries & lemons, but the delicate color & flavor provided by the blackberries is closest to our hearts. This is best served in individual dishes or glasses, so let your own cupboard provide inspiration!

FROZEN BLACKBERRY MOUSSE SOUFFLÉS

(serves 8-12)

ingredients

blackberry puree

3 c	fresh OR frozen blackberries, thawed

gelatin

¼ c	water
½	package plain gelatin (~1 t)

soufflé base

3	egg yolks
1 c	strained blackberry puree
1 t	finely grated lemon zest
2 T	lemon juice, freshly squeezed
¼ c	sugar

whip whites

3	egg whites
¼ c	sugar

whip cream

1 c	heavy whipping cream

techniques

*place blackberries in the bowl of a food processor
*puree on hi til smooth mixture forms, ~2-3 min
*strain into a sm bowl to eliminate seeds
*measure 1 c of strained puree for this recipe

*put water into a sm metal measuring cup OR
  sm saucepan
*sprinkle gelatin on top & allow to gel, ~ 5 min
*heat mixture gently, stirring, til gelatin
  softens to a liquid
*set aside

*put yolks, puree, zest, juice & sugar in the bowl
  of a stand mixer (whisk)
*whisk on hi speed til very foamy (should ~double-
  triple in volume), ~5-7 min (hand mixer ~10-14 min)
*add gelatin mixture slowly while whisking

*place egg whites in a separate clean bowl
*whisk with a mixer til foamy
*add sugar gradually to whites while mixing
*whip whites to med peaks
*fold whites into blackberry soufflé base in
  3 additions

*place cream in a separate clean bowl
*whip cream to med peaks
*fold whipped cream in yolk mixture in 2 additions
*combine thoroughly til no streaks are visible
*pour into individual serving dishes OR
  one lg soufflé dish
*place into freezer til firm, at least 1 hr (up to 3 hrs
  for a single lg soufflé dish)
*remove from freezer & let come partially to
  temp, ~15 min prior to serving

f chef notes

*this recipe is very bowl-centric – make sure to wash bowl & whisk thoroughly for each stage
*can be made 24-36 hours in advance (& gingerly covered with plastic wrap once frozen)
*if making in individual ramekins, try making parchment collars to allow for height above the rim

denise norton

John once took me on a surprise trip to the cotswolds in england. There were several fun pub meals...oh, & I had sticky toffee pudding three times during our five-day trip (in the name of research, of course!). Over the years, we've taught STP so many times I've lost count, but it usually ends with someone asking if it's inappropriate to lick their plate!

STICKY TOFFEE PUDDING

(serves 8-10)

ingredients	techniques
1 T unsalted butter	*preheat oven to 375°
	*butter a 9x9" square baking dish
sponge cake	
¾ c packed pitted dates	*use a food processor to finely mince the dates
1 c water	*put dates & water in a sm saucepan
	*boil, turn off heat & let sit for ~5 min
2 t baking soda	*add baking soda to date mixture & stir
	(it will froth up)
6 T unsalted butter, cut in T's & softened	*put butter & sugar in a lg bowl
1 c packed dark brown sugar	*stir with a wooden spoon til well combined
2 eggs	*add eggs, one at a time, to butter mixture &
	mix each til well incorporated
	*add date mixture to butter mixture & stir thru
1 c flour	*sift flour into batter & add syrup & vanilla
2 T maple syrup	*whisk til just incorporated (do NOT overmix)
1 t vanilla extract	*pour batter into prepared baking dish
	*bake til top is set, cake is risen & it shrinks
	from the sides, ~20-25 min
	*remove from oven & let cool at least 20 min
sauce	
1 T cornstarch	*put cornstarch, salt & milk in a sm bowl
1/8 t fine sea salt	(this is called a slurry)
2 T whole milk	*mix til well combined
8 T unsalted butter	*put butter & brown sugar in a med saucepan
½ c packed dark brown sugar	*cook over med flame & whisk til smooth
½ t vanilla extract OR vanilla bean paste	*whisk vanilla & cream into pan
¾ c heavy whipping cream	*stir til sugar is dissolved & mixture is combined
	*remix slurry & add to mixture
	*whisk continuously til entire mixture boils
	*remove from heat
	*cut cake & slather with warm sauce

The dates CAN be minced by hand, but they are very sticky & have a chewy texture (& as far as we know there are no "tricks" to make it easier when using a knife). So, if possible, use the food processor as it makes this part of the cake a snap to do!

Think chocolate pudding for adults. Then, think licking the bottom of the serving dish when no one is looking! We bake this dessert often in our classes & it is always a huge hit. The two major techniques we highlight are tempering (drizzling the cream into the eggs slowly while whisking rapidly, making sure the hot cream does not cook the eggs) & the water bath (surrounding the ramekins with hot water to gently cook them). Don't forget that the little pots thicken as they cool, so when you pull them out of the oven, they should still have a little "wiggle" to them! Then it's chill, serve & devour! ❧

CHOCOLATE POTS DE CRÈME
(makes 4-6 ramekins)

ingredients	techniques
	*preheat oven to 350º
	*set individual ramekins into a roasting pan (use 4-6 oz ramekins)
	*boil a teakettle full of water
2 c heavy whipping cream	*heat cream in a sm saucepan til just barely steaming & bubbling just around the edges
	*remove cream from heat
¼ lb bittersweet chocolate, finely chopped	*add chocolate & espresso to cream
1 T instant espresso granules OR powder	*let sit for ~2 min
	*whisk to melt chocolate & to combine chocolate & cream
3 egg yolks	*put yolks, sugar & extract in a med heatproof bowl
¼ c sugar	*whisk to combine thoroughly
2 t vanilla extract	*temper in cream mixture slowly, whisking constantly
	*strain mixture into a pitcher or lg measuring cup with a lip
	*pour chocolate mixture into ramekins, leaving at least a ¼" lip
	*pour boiling water gently ~ ½ way up outside of ramekins to create a water bath
	*bake til custard is set but slightly quivering, ~30-40 min
	*remove ramekins from roasting pan
	*cool to room temp & serve (OR refrigerate ~1½ – 2 hrs & let stand at room temp ~30 min before serving)
some whipped cream &/or shaved chocolate	*top with whipped cream / shaved chocolate

These scones are a newer addition to our list of favorites, but one bite & you'll understand why we HAD to include them! Don't be tempted to cut the apple pieces too small, as they "smush" a bit in the mixing process & provide a delightful tangy burst of flavor when you eat them.

APPLE CHEDDAR SCONES

(makes ~8 generous scones, ~1 dozen smaller scones)

<u>ingredients</u>

<u>techniques</u>

*preheat oven to 375°
*line 2 sheet pans with parchment paper
*bake the apples first - while they are in the oven,
 mise en place the remaining ingredients

3	tart apples (~1¼-1½ lb), peeled & cored (see picture box below about cutting)	*cut each apple into 16 pieces (chunks, not slivers) *place apples in a single layer on one sheet pan *bake til dry to the touch (~1/2 baked), ~20 min *cool completely in fridge, ~20 min
1½ c	flour	*put flour, sugar, baking powder & salt in a med bowl
¼ c	sugar	
1½ t	baking powder	*whisk by hand to combine
1 t	fine sea salt	
6 T	unsalted butter, cold, cut into sm pcs	*put butter, cheese, cream & egg in the bowl of a stand mixer (paddle) & add cooled apples
1 c	grated sharp white cheddar cheese	*paddle on low ~60 sec
¼ c	heavy whipping cream	*continue mixing & quickly sprinkle flour mixture over top as it mixes, til dough just comes together (do NOT overmix)
1	egg	*turn out dough to lightly floured work surface

*turn / knead 3-5 times til dough comes together
*pat dough into ~1¼" thickness
*cut with round biscuit cutters OR use a knife &
 cut into triangles
*place scones on second sheet pan

1	egg + pinch salt, whisked	*brush tops with egg & sprinkle on sugar
2 T	demerara sugar (brown cane)	*bake til firm & lightly golden, ~25-30 min

*cool ~5 min on sheet pan
*transfer to wire rack to cool (if you can wait!)

When cutting the apples - cut straight down around the core, taking off opposite sides, then opposite sides again. Cut the lg 1st sides into 6 pieces each & the sm 2nd sides into 2 pieces each (total of 16 pieces from the apple).

flavour favorites

This is our adaptation of pumpkin pie & it's much easier to make than the traditional version. With it's cookie crumb base (hence no pie crust to make!) & it's "measure, dump & mix" filling, it can be quickly assembled. The taste hits a more sophisticated note, too, with the mocha twist. We make PMT every year in our thanksgiving 101 class & it's always met with expressions of yum!

PUMPKIN MOCHA TART

(makes one 11" tart)

ingredients

crust
10 oz	anna's ginger cookies OR dry cookies (i.e. graham cracker OR shortbread)
1 T	instant espresso granules OR powder
2 T	cocoa powder
8-10 T	unsalted butter, melted

filling
15 oz	can of pure pumpkin puree
¾ c	packed dark brown sugar
8 oz	crème fraîche
1 T	very finely minced candied ginger
1 t	ground cinnamon
¼ t	ground nutmeg
¼ t	fine sea salt
1/8 t	ground cloves
3	eggs

topping
¼ c	semi-sweet OR bittersweet chocolate, melted

techniques
*preheat oven to 350°
*line a sheet pan with parchment paper
*place an 11" removable bottom tart pan on sheet pan

*place cookies in a resealable plastic bag
*crush cookies into fine crumbs with meat mallet
  (alternatively use a food processor)
*put crumbs in a med bowl
*sprinkle espresso & cocoa powder over crumbs
*add butter as needed so crumbs hold together
  when squeezed (don't allow butter to ooze)
*press crumbs firmly into removable bottom
  tart pan (onto bottom)

*place all filling ingredients in a lg bowl
*whisk together til very smooth
*pour filling carefully into tart pan
*bake til filling is set, ~45-55 min
*remove from oven
*transfer tart carefully to a wire rack
*let cool ~1 hr, then remove sides of tart pan
*refrigerate tart til set, at least 1 more hr
  up to 1 day

*dip spoon in chocolate & drizzle over tart to
  form decorative stripes
*cut into wedges & serve

This is a wicked, sinful dessert. We have a group of sunday students who, based on trying this dish in one class, requested that we schedule an entire class of bread pudding recipes! An excellent feature of bread pudding is how flexible it can be – add a cut up banana & some chocolate chips & it takes it to 11! Oh, & we won't tell you how ridiculous it tasted that one time we mixed in some croissants with the bread...

CLASSIC BREAD PUDDING WITH WHISKEY SAUCE

(serves 8-12)

ingredients

1	loaf french bread, crust removed & bread diced (~6 c of diced bread)
6 T	unsalted butter, melted
4 c	whole milk
1 c	heavy whipping cream
1 t	ground cinnamon
1/8 t	ground cloves
1/8 t	ground nutmeg
5	eggs
4	egg yolks
1 c	sugar
pinch	fine sea salt
1 T	vanilla bean paste OR extract

techniques

*preheat oven to 375º

*put bread in a lg bowl
*toss with butter to lightly coat
*put bread into 9x13" ceramic baking dish

*put milk, cream & spices in a med saucepan
*heat over med flame
*turn off when film forms & tiny bubbles appear around the edges

*put eggs, yolks, sugar, salt & vanilla in a lg bowl
*temper in milk mixture slowly, whisking constantly
*pour liquid over bread to cover
*press bread down to let bread absorb custard
*let sit for ~15-30 min to let bread absorb custard
*boil a teakettle full of water
*put baking dish in a larger roasting pan
*pour boiling water gently ~½ way up outside of ceramic baking dish to create a water bath
*bake til custard is set but slightly quivering, ~35-40 min
*remove baking dish from roasting pan
*cool slightly
*make whiskey sauce while bread pudding is cooling
*portion bread pudding into serving dishes
*drizzle with whiskey sauce

f chef notes

*this is a very adaptable recipe – feel free to add ~1 c of: raisins, chocolate chips, diced bananas, dried cherries, dried apricots OR toasted walnuts or pecans
*the texture of the bread is important to the final dish – a finer crumb on the bread will yield a smoother more custard like bread pudding & a toothier, coarser crumb on the bread will yield a chewier texture
*leaving the crust on the bread is tasty too & gives the bread pudding a nice toothy texture – however, it will take longer for the custard to soak into the bread (at least an hour), so factor in some extra time!

WHISKEY SAUCE
(makes ~2½ c)

<u>ingredients</u>

1 T   cornstarch
¼ c   whiskey

2 c   heavy whipping cream
1 T   unsalted butter
2 t   vanilla bean paste
¼ c   sugar
1 T   light corn syrup

<u>techniques</u>

*put cornstarch & whiskey in a sm bowl
*stir to dissolve cornstarch (this is called a slurry)

*put cream, butter, vanilla, sugar & corn syrup in
  a med saucepan
*heat over med flame, stirring occasionally
*heat til bubbles form around edge of mixture
*remix slurry
*add slurry to cream mixture & whisk to combine
*heat til mixture boils, ~2 min
*remove from heat & serve warm

There is almost nothing as show-stopping as a homemade cake & we thought it a perfect ending to this book. Real, pronounceable ingredients, classic baking techniques, patience, & a bit of flair & you finish with a tasty, homemade, grown-up dessert experience. As the saying goes, this one takes the cake! ⌒

HOMEMADE YELLOW CAKE

(makes one double layer 9" round cake with 2" tall pans OR
one triple layer 9" round cake with 1½" tall pans)

ingredients		techniques
		*preheat oven to 350°
		*line 2-3 sheet pans with parchment paper
1 T	unsalted butter, cold	*butter bottom & sides of two 9" cake pans (pan height should be at least 2" tall) OR three 9" cake pans (if height is less than 2" tall)
2-3 T	flour	*line bottoms of pans with parchment circles
		*butter over parchment circles
		*flour cake pans lightly & tap out excess
		*place each cake pan on a sheet pan
4 c	cake flour	*sift all dry ingredients into a med mixing bowl
2 t	baking powder	*set aside
1½ t	baking soda	
1 t	fine sea salt	
2 c	buttermilk	*combine buttermilk & vanilla
2 t	vanilla bean paste OR extract	*set aside
16 T	unsalted butter, softened	*put butter & sugar into the bowl of a stand mixer (paddle)
2 c	sugar	*cream on hi til pale & fluffy, ~3-4 min
4	eggs	*add eggs to butter/sugar mixture, one at a time, beating on med speed & scraping bowl after each addition
		*blend til completely smooth
		*alternate adding dry ingredients & buttermilk (3 additions of dry, 2 of wet), on low speed, scraping sides down often
		*transfer batter into prepared pans
		*level with spatula & "rap" pan on counter to eliminate air bubbles
		*bake til golden & skewer inserted comes out clean, ~40-50 min
		*cool in pans ~10 min
		*run knife around edge & invert onto cooling rack
1	recipe chocolate sour cream icing (next page)	*cool cake completely before icing

This flavor of this icing skews a bit "adult" when you make it with both bittersweet chocolate & the espresso powder. We like that contrast with the sweet homemade yellow cake. That said, don't be afraid to taste it (ahem!) & sweeten it up to your liking using light corn syrup. As for presentation, the icing doesn't have to be perfectly smooth to make a picture perfect cake!

CHOCOLATE SOUR CREAM ICING

(ices a double layer 9" cake OR
use measurements in bold for a triple layer 9" cake)

ingredients

NOTE: if you are making a three-layer cake, use the measurements in bold

16 oz	semisweet OR bittersweet chocolate, chopped **(24 oz)**
2 t	instant espresso granules OR powder (optional) **(3 t)**
16 oz	sour cream, room temp **(24 oz)**
1/3-½ c	light corn syrup (use less if using semisweet chocolate, more if bittersweet) **(½ – ¾ c)**
1 t	vanilla extract **(1½ t)**

ice cake

1	recipe homemade yellow cake (previous page)
1	recipe chocolate sour cream icing

techniques

*bring ~1-2" of water to a boil in a double boiler
*turn off heat

*put chocolate & espresso powder in the top of the double boiler (do not let bowl touch water)
*let chocolate melt, stirring occasionally
*remove from double boiler once smooth
*cool mixture to lukewarm

*put "wet" ingredients in a lg bowl
*whisk by hand til well combined
*add tepid chocolate slowly while whisking til mixture comes together
*taste for sweetness & add more corn syrup as desired, ~1 T at a time
*let cool in the fridge til frosting is spreadable, ~30 min
*rewhisk before icing cake

*place 1st cake layer on a cardboard cake round OR flat plate
*place ~1 c icing on top
*use spatula (without lifting) to spread icing
*place 2nd layer atop 1st
*ice top of 2nd layer in similar manner
*repeat with 3rd layer (as needed)
*ice cake sides
*cut into wedges & serve

chef notes

*to make the cake more level, use a serrated knife to cut off a portion of the top of each cake (see pictures on the previous page)
*to make a "square" cake top with clean edges, invert one of the cakes for the top layer so that the nice clean "bottom" edge of the baked cake becomes the cake top

FLAVOUR-ISMS
GLOSSARY / CONVENTIONS

"	inches	hi	high
&	and	hrs	hours
~	about OR approximately	julienne	a thin knife cut creating long, thin strips similar to matchsticks
1-2 T	suggests a range to use for an ingredient – we generally recommend that you try the lower end of the range in the recipe first & add more after tasting	lg	large
		med	medium
aka	also know as	min	minutes
al dente	identifies the proper consistency for cooked pasta & vegetables, meaning firm to the bite (literally translated in italian "to the tooth")	onion	if no other color is indicated, onion designates a spanish OR yellow onion
		oz	ounce
an	as needed	pkg	package
c	cup	pt	pint
chiffonade	a very thin knife cut creating fine ribbons, ~1/16" thick	q	quart
combo	combination	quality	we use this adjective for a prepared ingredient (like ketchup or mayonnaise) to remind readers to review the ingredient list on the product – avoid those that contain too many preservatives, too much salt OR too many unknown additives (look for pronounceable real foods!)
egg	large egg		
fine sea salt	we recommend sea salt in our recipes – we find the flavor to be gentler & softer than iodized table salt, which can often have a metallic finish. If you don't have sea salt, don't fret…the recipes will still work!	S+P	salt & pepper
		sec	seconds
		sm	small
fond	the concentrated crusty bits at the bottom of a pan after a food has been seared or sautéed		

stock	numerous recipes in this book require beef, chicken OR vegetable stock – we recommend that you use a good quality product (read the ingredient list & steer clear of unpronounceable ingredients & high amounts of salt). Our favorite packaged stock is a concentrated paste produced by a company called more than gourmet – it boasts real ingredients, low sodium & can be hydrated on demand so there is little to no waste.
T	tablespoon
t	teaspoon
temp	temperature
til	until
tt	to taste

RECIPE INDEX

chronological

alphabetical

INDEX